Diana
The Story Behind Her Private Life

Contributing Writer
Richard Buskin

PUBLICATIONS INTERNATIONAL, LTD.

Louis Weber, C.E.O.
Publications International, Ltd.
7373 North Cicero Avenue
Lincolnwood, Illinois 60646

ISBN: 1-56173-878-6

Richard Buskin is a British journalist who has conducted interviews and written articles for a wide variety of publications, including the *Observer Magazine*, *Paris Match*, the *New York Post*, and the *Sydney Morning Herald*. His previous books include the biography *John Lennon: His Life and Legend* and *The Films of Marilyn Monroe*.

Special acknowledgements to the following people for their assistance: Sue Eardley, for her patience and skill in carrying out research and conducting interviews; Lowri Turner, Margaret Holder, Kathy Iuliucci, Zelda Westmeads, and Dr. Dorothy Rowe, for their information and insight with regard to the complex life of the Princess of Wales; and Raymonde Buskin, for her invaluable editorial assistance.

Contents

Introduction: The Troubled Princess

Diana, Princess of Wales, is one of the most public people in the world, and not simply because her husband, Prince Charles, is the heir to the British throne. The public is fascinated with her for many reasons. Her 1981 marriage into the royal family is certainly the preeminent of these reasons, but there are also Diana's undeniable physical charms; her deserved reputation as a caring, devoted mother; an antic wit that shows itself at delightfully inappropriate moments; her unselfish involvement with charitable endeavors; the immensely appealing way in which she symbolizes Great Britain.

Beyond all of this, there is a "little girl lost" aspect to Diana's story. Few people can resist a real-life soap opera, particularly when it brims with the sort of heartbreak and irony that is at the core of Diana's life. She was a child of privilege who suffered through the divorce of her parents; a beautiful girl who wished she had been born a boy, and who was overshadowed academically by her siblings; the leading player in a storybook romance; a fulfilled mother yet an unhappy, profoundly unfulfilled wife. Diana has everything and nothing, a bitter truth that

Diana, Princess of Wales, was a beautiful bride who seemed to be the luckiest girl in the world. She married a prince in a fairy-tale wedding, and was expected to live happily ever after in a world most of us can only dream of. Yet today, many sources claim that her happiness was very short-lived.

has manifested itself in the emotional cycle of overeating and purging called bulimia, and in a number of apparent suicide attempts. Some may say that the attempted suicides—which include a tumble down a flight of stairs, a bit of jabbing with a penknife—are not severe enough to be taken seriously. These cynics fail to see that the gestures were Diana's cries for help, the pathetic flailings of someone who feels abandoned and violated. What is it that has made Diana so desperately unhappy? Much of what follows in this book will provide a substantial clue, but we may never know the complete story. Despite all the attention from the media and the public, despite all the speculation about Diana's relative happiness and emotional state, her thoughts remain her own, private and unknowable to the rest of us. Certainly, they seem unknowable to Charles—or perhaps he just doesn't care.

There it is again: irony. The irony of a remote, preoccupied husband who seems unconcerned about

The relationship between Charles and Diana is a tempestuous one. How their marriage is going to end is a question pondered today by many.

4

The whole world was fascinated by the union of the prince and princess. It was the wedding of the century with a glass carriage, a 25-foot-long bridal veil, and a 255-pound wedding cake.

his wife's physical well-being and fragile emotional state. The melodrama is irresistible.

Things seemed so different on July 29, 1981. It was a Wednesday in England, and in 74 countries around the world more than 700 million people were glued to their television sets to witness Lady Diana Spencer's marriage to Charles, Prince of Wales. The fairy-tale metaphor is trite, used-up, yet inescapable, for the romance and splendor of that day hardly seemed a part of the real world. It was a prolonged moment of fairy-tale magic brought to a world that had convinced itself that it no longer believed in such fancies. Against its will, then, the world was enchanted by blonde, beautiful Diana; her indescribably gorgeous gown; the glass coach that carried her to St. Paul's Cathedral in London; the dashing prince; the glorious, sober pomp of the wedding ceremony. Magic was afoot in the world.

Sadly, though, the woman who wore the fabulous gown was a naive 20-year-old girl who probably had little idea of what she was getting into. Upon her attractive shoulders would fall not just the responsibilities of a wife, and later a mother, but the weighty burden of centuries of British royal tradition. More significantly, perhaps, she would bear the tradition of a nation that was no longer as powerful as it once was, a nation that needed her not simply as a wife to

its king, but as a living, hopeful reminder to the world that England still stood for something grand.

As Charles's wife, Diana would one day be the Queen of England, and the daily routine that would prepare her to fulfill that sobering role would be neither kind nor understanding. On that Wednesday in 1981, Diana Spencer ceased to be Diana Spencer. She became Diana, Princess of Wales, a creature who belonged to Great Britain and the world.

In the 11 years since her marriage, Diana has blossomed and grown. If she has found the going rocky, it has seldom been because of any lack on her part. The girlish Diana of 1981 has been replaced by a sophisticated, maturing beauty who tends to her public duties with dedication and proper respect for those aspects that she considers most worthy. A striking figure at nearly six feet in heels, the blue-eyed princess has invigorated the whole idea of royalty, bringing equal measures of glamour, gravity, and sass to her role. Although less than a century removed from stuffy Victorian England, Diana seems to have very little in common with that era of masterful British men and well-bred but subservient women.

But even in the proper Victorian age, British royalty suffered its share of predicaments and peccadillos. Edward VII, successor and son to Queen Victoria, was noted for his extramarital carryings-on, affairs that were hushed up and conveniently ignored. It was not until 1936 that the first major modern-day crack appeared in Britain's royal facade. That year, Britons were shocked, the rest of the world stunned, when King Edward VIII announced his plan to abdicate so that he could marry a commoner, a two-time divorcée named Wallis Simpson. Edward had done the unthinkable by placing a higher value on his private life than on his public one. More recently, Princess Margaret raised eyebrows when she carried on romances with Peter Townsend and Roddy Llewellyn, relationships that bracketed Margaret's relatively short-lived marriage to Anthony Armstrong-Jones, popularly known as Tony Snowdon.

Diana's arrival on the scene must surely have struck the people of Great Britain like a delicious, welcome breeze. The new princess was young, beautiful, guileless. A replay of Margaret's jaded behavior seemed remote. Diana was smart enough to take her role seriously yet sufficiently lighthearted to give the public a princess they could adore and laugh with.

Princess Diana's trendsetting choices in clothes, hats, hairstyles, and makeup have set new standards for women all over the world to try to emulate. Her interest in style has also been a great boon to the local fashion industry, since on official duties Diana only wears clothes designed by Britons.

Whether attired in formal gown or shorts and T-shirt, Diana was 100 percent princess, and her subjects ate her up like ice cream. That they have continued to do so in the face of an extravagant royal lifestyle that the public, as taxpayers, is paying for is a remarkable testament to the depth of Diana's appeal.

The press loves her too, although not necessarily for the same reasons as the public. Simply put, Diana *sells*. She means robust circulation for British newspapers, "legitimate" dailies and brazen tabloids alike. She's a can't-miss magazine cover girl, and she means big numbers to television programmers around the world, who eagerly transmit her image to viewers who can't get enough.

Much of this media coverage is just fluff, of course—often-thoughtless trivia that has no more weight than a shaft of light that passes through a pane of glass. Sometimes juicy and always lightweight, coverage of this sort is concerned mainly with the figurehead Diana, the glamour gal, and—increasingly—the suffering wife. What is often less vigorously reported is Diana's unselfish involvement with charitable causes that include such institutions as the Child Accident Prevention Trust, Help the Aged,

Diana found an outlet for her energies in charity work. Since she has always been good with children, she was the logical choice for patron of Dr. Barnardo's, Britain's largest child-care organization. According to the organization's director, Dr. Bill Beaver, the princess is a real hands-on benefactor.

the housing-related Guinness Trust, and Dr. Barnardo's, Britain's largest child-care institution.

The disease-related projects to which Diana has allied herself read like a list of the most-feared ailments of the age: deafness, blindness, and lung disease; cancer, meningitis, Parkinson's disease; drug abuse, leprosy, AIDS. And make no mistake: Diana does not regard these campaigns merely as diversions or photo opportunities. To the contrary, she's an active, tireless campaigner who goes out of her way to promote and encourage funding for each cause. Savvy enough to understand her power as a unique individual, Diana knows that something as simple as offering her ungloved hand to an AIDS patient can begin to educate the world, and do untold good.

Diana does not have to put forth this sort of effort. She does not have to go the extra mile, but because she does, she is beloved by the British public and admired by millions around the globe. Her actions are thoughtful and generous, and if the British people occasionally grumble about supporting the royal family, they surely grumble least of all about supporting Diana, Princess of Wales.

The princess's presence always brings a smile to everyone's face. Those who know Diana well say that she is an extremely friendly, sensitive woman who, although shy herself, really knows how to get people to open up and talk to her. That's one of the reasons why she is so popular with crowds and media alike.

Diana's story is fascinating and tumultuous. To look at it merely as soap opera, though, is to do its central player—a kind, painfully vulnerable woman—a great disservice. The story that will unfold in the pages that follow is a tale of glamour and privilege, but also a human story. Although aspects of Diana's existence are larger than life, her triumphs and heartbreaks are little different, in essence, from those enjoyed and suffered by anybody. Like most of us, Diana must face her demons and disappointments head-on, as she struggles to come to grips with roles, expectations, and emotions that threaten at times to overwhelm her.

Even though her marriage to Prince Charles appears to be on the rocks, Diana tries her best to give "the heir and spare"—Princes Harry and William—as much of a normal childhood as possible. It's apparently not easy, especially since Prince Charles and she have very different ideas on how to raise the boys.

Growing up with Diana

Not only was the Honourable Diana Frances Spencer born with royal blood in her veins, she was born with far more of it than her future husband. The baby girl who came into the world on July 1, 1961, could claim blood ties to King Charles I, Charles II, George IV, and James II. Never mind that many of these relationships are based on illegitimate bloodlines that arose thanks to the kings' mistresses. The fact remains that Diana's family tree is a royally illustrious one.

Many other of Diana's relations, if not all of royal blood, are plenty famous. These include former British prime ministers Sir Winston Churchill and Sir Alec Douglas-Home (now Baron Home of the Hirsel), Lawrence of Arabia, King Juan Carlos of Spain, the Aga Khan, and U.S. presidents George Washington, Calvin Coolidge, and Franklin Roosevelt.

Then there's the literary branch of Diana's family tree, which includes Samuel Pepys, Jane Austen, George Sand, Louisa May Alcott, George Orwell, Graham Greene, Ralph Waldo Emerson, Virginia Woolf—even Erle Stanley Gardner, creator of Perry Mason.

Diana, the third daughter of the Viscount and Viscountess Althorp, was born into an aristocratic family with a very impressive family tree. It was certainly a world of privilege, even though no one guessed how privileged this little girl would grow up to be.

The mind spins at the names, but there are more: philosopher Bertrand Russell, painter John Singer Sargent, and a whole host of notable celebrities: Humphrey Bogart, Rudolph Valentino, Lillian Gish, Orson Welles, Olivia de Havilland, Lee Remick, tycoon Nelson Bunker Hunt, Gloria Vanderbilt, and *Washington Post* editor Ben Bradlee.

Of course, famous ancestors are no guarantee of familial happiness. The truth of this was particularly vivid in Diana's case, for she was born to parents who wanted a son more than anything else. The Viscount and Viscountess Althorp, more familiarly known as Johnnie and Frances Spencer, had been married for seven years and had produced three children by the time Diana arrived in 1961. March 1955 brought the couple's first child, Sarah. Jane came along in 1957 and John in January of 1960. Tragically, the deformed baby boy lived for just ten hours, dealing his parents a devastating blow, as well as underlining the reali-

Diana had a very carefree childhood growing up at Park House. After her parents' divorce, however, life was not so easy. Diana blamed herself for her parents' unhappiness and became moody and rebellious. She did give maternal comfort to her younger brother, Charles, who missed his mother terribly.

10

The Honorable Frances Roche, daughter of Lord and Lady Fermoy, married Viscount Althorp on June 1, 1954, at Westminster Abbey in London. The society wedding was attended by the queen, Prince Philip, the Queen Mother, and other members of the royal family. The bride and groom are the parents of Diana, Princess of Wales.

zation that they had missed another opportunity to ensure the family title. Without a male offspring, Johnnie and Frances would see the Spencer earldom, its perks and riches, lost to distant relatives.

So it was that in the summer of 1961 the couple was absolutely convinced that their next child would be a boy. The possibility of a girl had been barely considered; indeed, no female names had been selected when the 7-pound, 12-ounce baby girl was born in an upstairs bedroom at the Spencer residence at Park House.

Although not unwelcome, Diana was hardly celebrated. Even her christening was second-rate, at least when contrasted to the ceremonies that attended her older sisters. Sarah's godmother was the Queen Mother; Jane's godfather was the Duke of Kent. No such luminary was asked to fill a similar role for Diana, and the baby's christening was attended only by the family's friends and neighbors. The supreme irony of all this benign neglect, of course, is that Diana would become the first Englishwoman in more than 300 years to marry an heir to the throne.

If Diana has survived this inauspicious beginning more or less intact, it's because of an inner fortitude that seems to have sprung largely from her American ancestors. Her great-great-grandfather was Frank Work, an Ohio clerk who later made millions as a stockbroker in 19th-century Manhattan. Violently opinionated, Work demanded that his children avoid

romantic liaisons with foreigners—mates would be American, or else. No idle threat, for "or else" meant that offending offspring would be completely cut out of their father's will.

Work had a particular loathing for aristocratic Europeans, so one can imagine his reaction upon learning that daughter Frances had traveled to Europe in 1881 to marry the future 3rd Baron Fermoy. He broke off friendly relations with "Fanny," but did relent ten years later, when his daughter's marriage fell apart and she returned to America with her children in tow. Daddy Frank's one proviso was that Fanny never, *ever* commit the same sin again. Apparently eager to get back in her father's good graces, Frances even agreed that her boys would remain in America and would become American citizens within 12 months of her father's death.

Things seemed to have come to a congenial resolution, but Fanny was nothing if not consistent—and headstrong. In 1905 she ran off with one Aurel Batonyi, a Hungarian horse trainer who labored for Frank Work. This marriage, too, sailed onto the rocks and after four years Fanny had to face her irate father a second time. Frank Work had a foolish consistency of his own, for he forgave his daughter for this indiscretion, too.

Work died in 1911, leaving a will that was less than acceptable to his Harvard-educated grandchildren, who immediately turned themselves to the task of getting the document overturned. They succeeded on the grounds that their grandfather had been "un-

Frances, the 18-year-old bride of Viscount Althorp, is seen leaving her parents' home at Wilton Crescent, Belgravia, with her father, Lord Fermoy. He died in 1955. The marriage of the Althorps was dissolved in 1969. Frances, Diana's mother, is now Mrs. Shand Kydd.

duly prejudiced against foreigners." A fortune of £12 million was theirs.

When Fanny's first husband died in 1920, one of her sons by him, Maurice Roche, ascended to the title of 4th Baron Fermoy. The young man settled in Britain, where he eventually became a Tory member of Parliament and Mayor of King's Lynn. Roche married Ruth Gill, the daughter of a Scottish army colonel, in 1931. At 46, Roche was apparently unperturbed by the fact that his bride's great-grandmother was the illegitimate daughter of a girl from Bombay and a British worker for the East India Company. Still, this was not the sort of family history that was bragged about or even revealed in the thirties.

King George V, undoubtedly unaware of the skeleton that rattled in the closet of the Baron's wife, offered the couple a home at Park House on the Royal Sandringham estate in Norfolk. It was here that Diana's mother, Frances, was born in 1936.

The origins of Diana's father, Johnnie, are less melodramatic but even more deeply steeped in royalty. Born 12 years before Frances, Johnnie was a godson of Queen Mary and part of a line of earls, dukes, and duchesses that could be traced back to the 15th century. King George III bestowed the title of Earl Spencer on one of Johnnie's 18th-century ancestors. In time, the title came to Johnnie's father, Jack Spencer, who married the beautiful Lady Cynthia Hamilton. Her sweet nature was in sharp contrast to Jack Spencer's violent temper and sadistic streak.

The enormous Althorp House was a magnificent and glamorous home for Diana and her siblings. When their father married Raine, the ex-wife of the ex-Earl of Dartmouth, she set out to completely change its look. The Spencer children were up in arms when paintings were sold, wall-to-wall carpeting was laid, and admission to visit was charged.

The couple's son, Johnnie, was educated at Eton and Sandhurst. He grew to be an amiable, easygoing man who served with the Royal Scots Greys in World War II and later began a political career in postwar South Australia. After his return to England, Johnnie became equerry (personal attendant) to King George VI in 1950, positioning himself to become Master of the Queen's House when the king died in 1952.

The privileged are no less prone to the vagaries of the human heart than anyone else, so Johnnie can probably be excused for falling for Frances Roche while he was engaged to somebody else. His intended, Lady Anne Coke, was given her freedom not long after Johnnie met Frances, who was 18 years old and every bit as headstrong as her great-grandfather, Frank Work.

Frances's June 1, 1954, wedding to the Viscount Althorp was held at Westminster Abbey and was *the* British society event of 1954. The ceremony attracted

When Diana's grandfather died in June 1975, her father was elevated to the 8th Earl Spencer. Brother Charles became the Viscount Althorp, and Diana and her sisters became ladies. The family also moved from their beloved Park House to Althorp (above), a splendid estate on 13,000 acres.

After their parents' separation, Diana and brother Charles went to London with their mother. When their father gained custody, they returned to Park House to live with him and their maternal grandmother, Lady Ruth Fermoy. Diana tried to act as surrogate mother to young Charles in their mother's absence.

1,500 guests, including Queen Elizabeth, Prince Philip, the Queen Mother, and Princess Margaret. Frances was the youngest bride to walk down the famed Abbey's aisle in the 20th century. By any standard, then, the marriage of the people who would become Diana's parents had got off to an auspicious, even glorious, beginning.

But there was trouble in paradise, and not just the agony of waiting for a son. As the years rolled by, Johnnie and Frances discovered that they just weren't compatible. Johnnie enjoyed the unambitious life of a country squire, an existence defined mainly by hunting and similar masculine but lightweight pursuits. Frances, on the other hand, was an ambitious person who enjoyed the London social life, and had a keen understanding of the importance of sociability. Worse, Frances was convinced that Johnnie took her for granted, and used her mainly as a sounding board for his often argumentatively expressed opinions.

The couple's longtime quest for a son hardly helped the relationship. Although a son, Charles (godson to the queen), was finally born in May of 1964, too much damage had been done for the marriage to thrive. Diana and the other children still remained oblivious to the friction that had built up between their parents, but they would not remain oblivious for long.

For the time being, though, life for the children at Park House was idyllic. Proper care was provided

by a nanny and six servants. The ten-bedroom house had an outdoor swimming pool, a tennis court, a cricket pitch, and cottages for the staff. It was a rambling, informal place where Diana and her siblings were relaxed and content. Indeed, Diana's earliest memories are of the lovely grounds and the variety of animals that roamed there.

In some ways, Diana's early life was hardly different from that of other children in Britain or America. Although she was taught at home by a governess from the age of four, she and the other children also adored the Beatles and were allowed to fill one room with Fab Four memorabilia. In some aspects, then, Diana was a typical little girl.

Although she had no grasp of the privileged nature of her existence, Diana did come to understand by about the age of five that things were seriously wrong between her parents. The agonizing slide to Frances and Johnnie's final break was precipitated by a friend's innocent dinner party in 1966, where Frances and Johnnie were introduced to Peter and Janet Shand Kydd. Peter Kydd, a businessman and former naval officer, was bright, witty, and fun to be around. He was the antithesis of Johnnie in many ways, and it seems almost inevitable that Frances was attracted to him.

The two couples became friendly and often socialized together. During a ski vacation, Janet Kydd

Diana's mother left her first husband, Johnnie Spencer, after getting involved with Peter Shand Kydd. She never thought she would lose custody of her four children. Her mother, Lady Ruth Fermoy, however, testified against her, prompting the courts to award custody to her ex-husband. Frances has never forgiven her mother.

realized that her husband and Frances were enjoying each other far more than they were enjoying the powdered slopes. Before the ski trip was over, nearly everyone in the Spencers' social circle was aware of the incipient love affair—everyone, that is, except poor Johnnie.

Later, secret meetings between Kydd and Frances in fashionable sections of London came to Johnnie's attention, and it became clear to all that the marriage was in deep trouble. Peter Kydd decided to leave his wife and three children, and Frances moved from Park House to an apartment in London's exclusive Belgravia district. Diana's elder sisters, Sarah and Jane, had left for boarding school just days before their mother departed from Park House. But Diana and younger brother Charles were swept up in the middle of all the activity, joining their mother at the Belgravia digs a day after Frances moved in. Diana was enrolled in day school, and Charles was sent to kindergarten.

The break with Park House and Johnnie was not total, however: For the moment, the Althorps had agreed to a trial separation, and the children continued to visit Park House on weekends. But despite a family get-together at the big house during Christmas, 1967, Frances realized there was no turning back. The marriage was over.

As happens so often in divorce cases that involve children, a tug-of-war developed over custody, with Diana and her brother and sisters cast in the role of the rope. Predictably, Frances wanted the children to live with her; just as predictably, Johnnie swore that his offspring would never live beneath the same roof as his unfaithful wife and her lover. Confident that her adultery was not an issue because she had never abused or neglected her children, Frances instigated legal proceedings to gain custody. Although the British courts usually can be relied upon to award custody to the mother, in this case Frances was simply outclassed by the weight of her husband's name, title, and connections. Making the contest even more difficult for Frances was the negative intervention of her mother, Ruth, Lady Fermoy, who took Johnnie's side and urged the court to award him custody.

And that is what the court did. The outcome was a bitter blow to Frances and precipitated a deep, permanent rift with her mother.

Janet Shand Kydd had sued Peter for divorce in the meantime (grounds: adultery), freeing him to

Diana had a marvelous life at Park House as a small girl. There were grounds to explore, siblings to play with, and pets to befriend. The pool and tennis courts provided many hours of relaxation and fun. It was there that Diana became an excellent swimmer—a sport she enjoys to this day.

marry Frances. Following an April 1969 divorce decree granted to Johnnie, Frances wed Peter Kydd the following month. Frances had got what she wanted, with the not unexpected side effect of a bunch of confused, miserable kids.

None of the children was more upset than Diana, whose personality did an about-face into rebelliousness and hyperactivity. Still, she did give maternal comfort to little brother Charles, who missed his mother terribly. As for the other children, Jane became moody and withdrawn, and Sarah decided she would ignore all rules of discipline.

Park House seemed to reverberate with the echoes of the children's mother, whose absence was all the more obvious when Diana and the other children had to say good-bye to her at the end of their weekend visits. The emotional confusion wrought by the divorce expressed itself in the children's bad behavior, which in turn led to an alarming turnover in nannies, many of whom simply threw up their hands after unsuccessful attempts to control the gaggle of defiant, disruptive children.

Diana and the others were clearly acting out; one does not have to be a clinical psychologist to realize that this period of Diana's life was immensely damaging to her, and probably planted the seeds of loneliness and insecurity that bedevil her today.

The next difficult stage in Diana's life was boarding school, a place in Norfolk called Riddlesworth

West Heath School in Kent was Diana's home from 1973 to 1977. There she developed the reputation of being a very friendly, popular girl. Unfortunately, her academic record was poor. She failed every single O-level exam she took and abruptly ended her academic career.

Hall, to which she was sent 18 months after her parents' divorce. Although initially convinced that she was being packed off and rejected, Diana soon settled in at the large, aristocratic country house. She became a popular and outgoing student who excelled in team sports, and who became known as a girl who was cooperative and helpful.

Riddlesworth emphasized a traditional curriculum that included English, French, Latin, history, mathematics, and the sciences. Diana enjoyed writing essays and had an interest in history, but it soon became clear to all—including Diana—that academics were not her strong suit, and that she would never match the academic achievements of her brother and sisters.

Diana was hit hard by the 1972 death of her grandmother, Countess Spencer, but the tall 12-year-old did sufficiently well in her Common Entrance exam the following year to gain admittance to the West Heath boarding school. Sarah and Jane had already studied at this large Georgian mansion set in 32 acres in the Kent countryside. Apparently unimpressed, Diana endured the place for six weeks and pronounced herself completely miserable. It was thanks mainly to the intervention of Ruth Rudge, the school's kindly headmistress, that Diana was persuaded to stay on.

A challenging rite of passage in the British educational system is the "O level" ritual, which students usually undertake at age 16. These "ordinary level" exams are designed to indicate the student's fitness to progress to higher education in selected subjects. Diana's sister Sarah had passed six O levels, despite being suspended from West Heath for rebellious-

ness and drinking. Jane, more steady and reserved than Sarah, had passed 11. But when Diana took five O levels—in history, geography, English language and literature, and art—she failed them all. A second attempt brought just one passing mark, in art. By the time her West Heath career ended in 1977, she had established herself as a willing, well-liked, yet unaccomplished student. Although she was appointed school prefect and won the Miss Lawrence Clark Award for service to the school, her disappointing academic performance at a place that cost £3000 a semester must surely have caused a major rent in her self-esteem.

Diana's grandfather died in June 1975, and Johnnie was elevated to the title of the 8th Earl Spencer. Brother Charles became the Viscount Althorp, and Diana and her sisters became ladies. Most significant from Diana's point of view was a move from the beloved Park House to the traditional Spencer residence at Althorp.

For a while, the move did not bring with it any traumatic side effects. Althorp was an enormous, magnificent house that was built in 1508 and renovated in the late 18th century. The total estate was some 13,000 acres, an hour's drive north of London. The house was situated in the middle of a gorgeous 600-acre park. Inside, the place was eye-popping: marble floors, crystal chandeliers, gorgeous tapestries. All this, plus paintings by Rubens, Gainsborough, Van Dyck, and other masters. Diana and her siblings were understandably impressed by the splendor and awhirl with the seeming glamour of it all. Diana explored the grand house eagerly and with fascination, but found particular pleasure in her second-floor bedroom, where she happily amused herself by reading light novels. One of her favorite writers was romance novelist Barbara Cartland, whose only daughter, Raine, Countess of Dartmouth, would soon enter Diana's life in a surprising and most unwelcome way.

Not long after moving into Althorp, Johnnie began an affair with Raine. A year later, in 1976, Raine's husband, Lord Dartmouth, sued her for divorce on the grounds of adultery. Shortly after that, on July 14, 1976, Johnnie and Raine were wed at the Caxton Hall registry office in London. Diana and the

After their parents' divorce, Diana and her siblings spent many school vacations in Scotland, on the Isle of Seil near Oban, with their mother and her new husband. Here the children spent their days mackerel fishing and looking for lobsters.

Diana's oldest sister, Sarah, was a much better student than Diana. She passed six O levels, but was suspended from West Heath at age 16 for drinking. It was she who actually introduced the young Diana to Charles in 1977 when he came up to Althorp for a shooting vacation.

other children were not present at the ceremony; they did, in fact, not even know about it. So Diana's life had once again been changed by a circumstance that she was powerless to resist.

The Spencer children got on badly with Raine from the start. Their new stepmother was a tall, formidable woman who favored gaudy clothes and bouffant hairdos. Extroverted and outspoken, she fondly called her new husband "Johnnikins" but could be depended upon to make the occasional hurtful remark to other people. The children were undoubtedly confused when Raine began to sell off Althorp's treasures in order to raise cash, and further confused when she opened the house to the public as a money-making tourist attraction.

More than the commercialization of Althorp (which shocked many Britons), Diana and the other children were put off by Raine herself. They didn't like her looks, they didn't like her bossiness, they didn't like her connection to their father. If Raine was outspoken, the children matched her, making no secret of their disdain for her. She returned their antipathy, and the household was soon awash in bad feeling. "Raine, Raine go away," became a familiar litany in the great halls of Althorp; likewise "Raine stopped play." Even the servants got into the act, for when Raine described a couple of kitchen workers as "a pair of sluts," the servants sourly declared, "It never Raines, but it pours."

Jokes of this sort may provoke a certain uneasy amusement, but the situation was no joke to Diana, who had endured the breakup of her parents, a dis-

appointing academic career, disorienting moves from one household to another, the deaths of grandparents, and now an overbearing, unloving stepmother. Diana repeatedly defied Raine, and Charles did likewise. Jane acted as though her stepmother were invisible and Sarah was unapologetically hostile to her.

Never one to hide her feelings, Raine has given as good as she got, publicly describing Jane as "only good for producing children" and dismissing Sarah as "okay while she sticks to hunting and shooting, which is all she cares about." As for Diana—well, Raine has fallen most cruelly on her, rhetorically asking, "How can you have a conversation with someone who doesn't have a single O level? It's a crashing bore."

As Diana and her sisters grew older, they spent less time at Althorp. Although they adored their father, Raine was simply too much to bear. Diana eventually chose to avoid her stepmother altogether by staying in London with her sisters on weekends.

A more definite reprieve was granted Diana in 1978, when she left England after being enrolled in Switzerland's Institut Alpin Videmanette, an exclusive finishing school where she had been preceded by Sarah. Ostensibly a place where Diana would learn dressmaking, cooking, and "domestic science," the Institut was really just a place where Diana could ski with an English friend, Sophie Kimball. But six weeks of Sophie and the slopes were enough for Diana, who grew bored and returned home. Not surprisingly, she avoided Althorp and Raine by moving in with her mother in London.

At 16, gangly but with rapidly developing beauty, Lady Diana Spencer had chucked one sort of life and was anxious to find another. Not far away, a young prince was looking for something, too.

Hoping to get some peace from the press, Lady Diana Spencer agreed to pose with two of the children from the Young England kindergarten in St. George's Square in 1980. What she did not expect, however, was the stir caused by her transparent voile skirt showing her legs for the whole world to see. Prince Charles was supposedly greatly amused by the whole episode.

The Man Who Would Be King

Anyone interested in the solemn aspect of royal life in 20th-century Britain would do well to study an English newsreel that dates from 1957. In it, a nine-year-old boy named Charles arrives for his first day at Cheam, an exclusive, very traditional boarding school in Headley. He's a solemn little fellow with erect posture; quick to raise a respectful cap to his teachers and apparently unmoved by the fuss that swirls around his arrival. His parents are with him for this first day at the new place—his father, Prince Philip, and his mother, Elizabeth II, Queen of England. The little boy, of course, is Charles, Prince of Wales, and he is being formally greeted at Cheam because his birthright is the English throne. It is assumed by all present at the school, and by all who will watch this bit of newsreel, that the serious little boy will one day be the King of England.

Charles's parents would depart not long after the filmed arrival, leaving the boy with the other students, with the detective-bodyguard assigned to look after him, and with his own thoughts. During those first days at Cheam, Charles's thoughts were lonely, miserable. His relationship with his strong-willed father kept him on guard constantly, and now he had been abandoned at this strange place.

On July 1, 1969, Charles, the oldest son of Queen Elizabeth II and Prince Philip, was officially invested as the 21st Prince of Wales at Caernavon Castle. The ceremony was partly in English and partly in Welsh. That same day, Diana, the future Princess of Wales, celebrated her eighth birthday. Opposite: Young Charles

The boy accepted his "abandonment" rather quickly, but still had to deal with the unending prying of the press, with the expectations of his parents and teachers, and with an awareness that the other boys expected him to be "interesting."

Unfortunately, young Charles seemed ill-equipped to shine in any area. Although described in biased press reports as "bright" and "above average," he was in truth a bit of an academic plodder at Cheam, fond of history and geography, poor in mathematics and foreign languages. His father, Philip, had not been much of a student during his own tenure at Cheam, but he had been a strong presence on the athletic field, excelling in cricket, rugby, and soccer. Charles was bored by cricket and ineffective at rugby. And although he did become captain of the school's soccer team, the squad lost every one of its games—and by lopsided margins, at that. The boy seemed to be, well, undistinguished.

Yet Charles was made of stronger stuff than even he may have realized. In time, he grew to be a self-assured, intellectually active man who knew his own mind, and who had a clear sense of his place in history, and of his responsibility to Britain. He was very different from Diana, and if their eventual marriage was not inevitable, clashes almost certainly were.

Prince Charles was christened in Buckingham Palace on December 15, 1948. His robe was designed by Prince Albert for Queen Victoria's first-born child. Queen Mary, his great-grandmother, is seen holding the young prince here.

Charles's life story is not one of the idle rich, nor is it a gaudy tale of the self-indulgent *nouveaux riches*. Rather, it is a story of a life of privilege and a life-long preparation to assume great, even grave, responsibility. Although British monarchs are now essentially powerless, their symbolic value and historical weight are almost inestimable. They no longer significantly affect the course of history but are very prominent within it. For this reason, Charles's story becomes important indeed.

On November 14, 1948, at about 9:15 P.M., the future Prince of Wales became the first royal baby to be born at Buckingham Palace in 62 years. From the moment of his birth, then, Charles was doing significant things. London echoed with 21-gun salutes and the British people, living gray lives in a nation that was not close to recovering from the savage economic and human losses of World War II, celebrated joyously, spontaneously. People danced in the streets and the flicker of bonfires illuminated modest homes and storefronts. The baby boy was the first direct successor to the throne since the uncrowned Edward VIII.

In the hours immediately preceding the birth, physicians solicitously attended to Princess Elizabeth, who endured the effort and discomfort of incipient childbirth. Prince Philip found the waiting a bit of a trial and retired to the palace swimming pool and squash court with a male friend. The news of the baby's birth was delivered to Philip on the court.

Charles missed seeing his father altogether at the moment of his birth, and would see relatively little of Philip throughout his childhood. At about the time of Charles's first birthday, Philip left his post at the Admiralty in London for active naval duty.

Elizabeth, too, became preoccupied with duties of her own, particularly as the health of her father, King George VI, deteriorated, forcing the princess to assume many of his duties. Charles's sister, Anne, was born in August of 1950, and from that point the two children spent most of their time together, under the tutelage of nannies. Their mother would spend 30 minutes with them each morning, and another hour or two in the latter part of each afternoon.

The family was not an unloving one, yet there was a distinct air of formality to the relationships. Tiny Charles was taught to bow before his great-grandmother, Queen Mary, and to stand unless permitted otherwise when in the presence of his grandfather, the king. It was these relatives, in fact, that Charles saw more than his parents, both of whom were busy with much of the royal protocol that the ailing King George could no longer attend to. A lifetime of smoking had taken its toll on the monarch,

In August of 1951, the royal family spent some time together at Clarence House after Prince Philip's return from Royal Navy maneuvers. Left to right are Charles (2½ years old), Prince Philip, Anne (1 year old), and Princess Elizabeth.

22

and though he was only in his mid-fifties, he was dying of a cancer that he had still to be informed about.

Prince Philip was forced to give up his naval command in the summer of 1951 in order to devote still more time to working with his wife. On February 6, 1952, while Elizabeth was staying at the Treetops hunting lodge next to Kenya's Sagana River, an aide fell to one knee and addressed the 25-year-old princess as "Your Majesty"; Elizabeth knew that the cancer had carried her father away and that she would now give herself totally to the life for which she had been prepared since her birth.

The young queen and her family moved into Buckingham Palace on Easter Sunday, 1952. Their former residence, Clarence House, would henceforth be the home of the king's widow and his younger daughter, Margaret.

For three-year-old Charles, the move meant his own car and chauffeur, his own footman, and the first of an unending series of detective-bodyguards who would shadow his every move for the rest of his life. The child also gained a new title: Duke of Cornwall.

Charles took public events—even the June 1953 coronation of his mother—in stride, yet remained basically shy. He was a sensitive child who tried early on to emulate his father's aggressiveness, but who realized that he was simply not cut from the same cloth as Philip.

Elizabeth, more sensitive than Philip to Charles's demeanor, felt that the boy was becoming withdrawn, even nervous. Rather than send him away to school, the queen resolved to have him tutored at the palace, in a room specially set aside for study.

Charles and his entourage did go out, of course, and when they did attention from the press was inevitable. No matter the venue—a museum, an athletic field, a public ceremony—the boy was legitimately regarded as news. If the press did not exactly prey on him, neither was it gentle, and in time Elizabeth had to appeal to the press to exhibit a bit of restraint.

A British heir to the throne had never attended a normal school, but in 1956 Elizabeth was ready to break with the centuries-old tradition. Charles would continue to be tutored at home in the mornings but would join his class at Hill House private school in London's Knightsbridge each afternoon. A year later, Charles was attending Hill House on a full-time basis.

As children, Charles and Anne saw little of their mother. They spent most of their time in each other's company under the tutelage of nannies. From an early age, Charles was quiet and sensitive; his sister was gregarious and headstrong.

Although his teachers addressed him as Prince Charles, his fellow students were not expected to use the title.

At this time, Philip made a conscious effort to mold Charles in his own image. The Duke of Edinburgh was a strict, forceful man who was quick to punish, slow to praise. He encouraged his son to participate in sports and hoped for outstanding results that, alas, were not forthcoming. Instead of his father's beloved soccer and rugby, Charles was more interested in swimming and fly-fishing. The boy also enjoyed painting, reading, and a pastime new to future kings: watching television.

Charles's subsequent career at Cheam was marred not only by his so-so academic and athletic performance, but by the increasingly aggressive presence of the press. Photographers seemed to be constantly underfoot, and reporters stooped to offering bribes to Charles's schoolmates for little bits of information or gossip. At the close of Charles's first semester at Cheam, the queen's press secretary warned that if the intrusive behavior did not stop, the prince would be withdrawn from school and educated in the isolation of Buckingham Palace.

Charles's father, Prince Philip, insisted that his son be sent to Gordonstoun, a school in Scotland that he himself had attended. The young prince had a difficult time adjusting.

The press agreed to conduct itself with more moderation and things might have turned out all right except that Charles's time at Cheam came to a natural end and it was time for him to move on—and just when he had finally acclimated himself to the place. His mother assumed that his next stop would be Eton, the traditional place of education for upperclass boys. Philip had other ideas. He reasoned that Eton, barely more than a stone's throw from Windsor Castle, would only encourage the press's attention to Charles. Philip suggested Gordonstoun, a Scottish school located on the North Sea far from the family home, yet still within the British Isles. And it was surely no coincidence that Philip himself had attended Gordonstoun; once again, he was attempting to mold Charles into a likeness of himself.

If daily existence at Cheam had been challenging, it was positively unbearable at Gordonstoun, where Charles was thrown into a grueling regimen of mountain climbing, firefighting, and lifesaving; dashes through assault courses; and a pore-opening routine of long runs and cold showers. Woe unto the boy who refused to participate, or who did so ineffectually, for he would be admonished by his teachers and ostracized by his peers.

Charles tried desperately to blend in with the group at Gordonstoun—not easy considering his title and the fact that his bodyguard never went away. Unlike the boys at Cheam, the Gordonstoun students were inclined to keep their distance, so Charles passed a great deal of time alone (with his shadow in tow, of course), taking introspective strolls along the blustery coastline. At 14, he wanted, and needed, to grow socially, to make friends and blossom as a person. That this opportunity was denied him was a source of considerable frustration to him. After the press exaggerated a minor escapade in a local bar, the boy hated his existence more than ever.

Vacation interludes at home with his parents were hardly more serene. Charles and Philip frequently argued and the boy sometimes ended up in tears. But Charles's latent strength of character was beginning to come to the fore: It is rumored that during one argument with his father, Charles curtly reminded Philip that he was addressing the future King of England; with that, Philip turned on his heel and walked out of the room.

Queen Elizabeth II and Prince Philip have been married since November 20, 1947. Their relationship seems to have been a good one through the years. She attends to more royal duties. He is the chief decision-maker in the household.

At Cambridge, the young Charles studied archaeology and anthropology during his first year; history the next two years. Charles believed a generalist route was befitting a future King of England, who had duties to Crown and country.

The press continued to hound Charles, publishing unauthorized extracts from his examination books, then claiming that the boy had sold other exam books to classmates when he needed spending money. These allegations aside, Charles was making academic progress—so much that by 1965, at 16, he passed his O-level exams, signaling his readiness to move on to a higher level of education. In addition, he had gained a measure of acceptance among the other Gordonstoun students because of acclaimed performances in school music and dramatic productions.

From this point, Charles's life improved steadily, dramatically. He convinced his parents to let him take a break from Gordonstoun in order to study at Timbertop, a demanding school in the Australian outback, 200 miles north of Melbourne in the Victorian Alps. There, the older students learned to become ruggedly self-reliant, and proficient in hunting, cooking, and woodcutting. They organized their own schedules and looked after the younger boys.

Charles arrived at Timbertop in January of 1966. From the start, he felt at home amid the simple surroundings and with the other students. He lived in the school's compound of huts and performed his

fair share of household chores. He hiked and ran cross-country; he felled trees and sheared sheep; he panned for gold and even found time to study for the demanding "A-level" (advanced-level) examinations required for entry to college. By the time he finished at Timbertop, he had impressed students and faculty alike with his dedication and general hardiness.

The triumph was an important one for Charles, who felt for the first time that he had been accepted for who he was rather than for what he was. He had put himself to the test and had passed, defining himself in the process. Back home in England, he discovered a newfound confidence when dealing with crowds, and an increased willingness to talk and mingle with the people. In an odd twist, the boy born in England became a man in Australia.

Having returned to study at Gordonstoun, the prince blossomed academically. He cultivated interests in opera, classical music, and archaeology, and attained A-level passes in French and history. No small accomplishment, the latter, for Charles thus became

Prince Charles qualified for a pilot's license at the age of 21. He obtained his wings as a jet pilot at Royal Air Force College in Cranwell. The prince's grandfather, George VI, had been the first member of the royal family to fly with the RAF.

the first-ever heir to the British throne to qualify for college study by conventional means.

By now 18 years old, Charles could ascend to the throne immediately if the need arose, without the government having to provide a temporary replacement.

Charles began university study at Trinity College, Cambridge, in the fall of 1967, intending to pursue a three-year degree course in archaeology and anthropology. In America, students were just coming off the drug-induced high of the Summer of Love, and students in Western Europe were little different. Charles resisted this quest for the bold and new, maintaining his studies and upholding traditional values, in the classroom and out of it. He mingled mainly with the landed gentry and immersed himself in the decidedly unradical sport of polo.

Before the beginning of his second year at Cambridge, Charles switched to an emphasis in history. Prior to his July 1, 1969, investiture as Prince of Wales, he studied Welsh for a month at the University College of Wales.

When Charles completed his studies at Cambridge in 1970, the 21-year-old became the first-ever heir to the throne to have gained an honors degree. From this success he went into the Royal Air Force, plunging into the world of jet fighters and bombers and earning his RAF wings. While serving aboard Royal Navy ships and nuclear submarines, Charles learned about bravery and comradeship firsthand, and discovered the intangible rewards that come with the successful accomplishment of difficult tasks.

One step at a time, then, in increasingly challenging, increasingly male-dominated environments, Charles's mature personality was formed. Although more intellectually accomplished than his father and not quite as dogmatic, Charles nevertheless came to share with Philip a belief in the value of ambition and discipline. And like Philip, Charles came to believe in the traditional, aristocratic way of raising children: firmly, seriously, and often through the intervention of hands other than those of the parents.

Wedded to royal tradition, keenly aware of his present and future roles, and satisfied with his accomplishments, Prince Charles was a young man who placed his duties to his country above all else. To countless millions, though, he was Charles, eligible bachelor. As soon as the boy became the man, speculation about his romances began, grew, and

Prince Charles's background is steeped in military service. He took courses at the Royal Naval College, the Royal Air Force College, and the Royal Marines. He is also the first heir to the throne to make a parachute landing.

eventually threatened to overwhelm all other aspects of his public life. The birthdays passed by and still Charles remained unattached, unmarried. Did any woman in Britain possess the right combination of birth, beauty, and brains to win this paragon? Who would it be, and when would the people of Britain know her?

Charles was in no hurry to provide an answer, but when it came, it delighted all of Britain and much of the world.

Courtship and Conquest

Now in her early thirties, Diana has known her husband for nearly half her life. On the November day in 1977 that the couple first met, the prince was romancing Diana's older sister, Sarah. The British press had speculated about the depth of Charles's attachment to the elder Lady Spencer, as it had speculated about his regard for the many women who had preceded her. Interestingly, though, it was Sarah herself who arranged Charles's meeting with her younger sister.

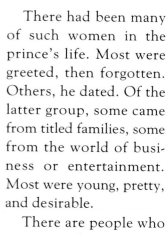

The official announcement of the engagement of Charles and Diana took place on February 24, 1981. The lord chamberlain, Lord Maclean, made the announcement to a roomful of guests at Buckingham Palace. Opposite: Diana learned that living the life of a princess would be very different from what she was used to.

There had been many of such women in the prince's life. Most were greeted, then forgotten. Others, he dated. Of the latter group, some came from titled families, some from the world of business or entertainment. Most were young, pretty, and desirable.

There are people who will insist that Charles is by nature a Casanova, an inveterate lothario who happily sets his sights on particular women the way a child eyes the goodies in a bakery window. There are others who claim that the prince, in his bachelor days, was merely exercising the right of single men to play the field, to gain the experience that would help him choose a mate wisely, sensibly.

Was she anxious to extricate herself from a relationship she found unsatisfying, or was she selflessly playing matchmaker on Diana's behalf?

The questions, at least as things stood in 1977, are moot, for Diana was at the time a shy, slightly overweight 16-year-old with relatively little to offer Charles, a sophisticated man of 29. Still, the life of a prince involves endless meetings and hellos, so when Charles first laid eyes on Diana, in the middle of a plowed field at Althorp during a weekend pheasant shoot, he greeted her pleasantly. And when the encounter had passed, Diana was most likely filed in Charles's memory as just another sweet-faced young woman of good birth.

Charles's first real romance dates from his days at Trinity College, Cambridge, in the late 1960s. The woman was Lucia Santa Cruz, the first in a field of women whose backgrounds run the gamut of the British class system. In 1972 there was Georgiana Russell, daughter of a British ambassador to Spain. Later came Lady Jane Wellesley, daughter of the 8th Duke of Wellington. She and Charles were constant companions for three years.

Charles has been smitten not only with high-born ladies, but with glamorous women from the world

Beer heiress Sabrina Guinness was once romantically linked to Prince Charles. She had also had a relationship with Mick Jagger and was nanny to Ryan O'Neal's daughter, Tatum. Her visit to Balmoral was purported to be a disaster—the queen and Prince Philip were rude to her and Charles ignored her.

of entertainment. One of these was film actress Susan George, whose performances have been distinguished mainly by her willingness to shed her clothes. Another was entertainer Sheila Ferguson, lead singer of the all-girl pop group, the Three Degrees. Clearly, Charles's relationships with both women were mere dalliances, as neither would be acceptable as his wife.

Certain women were unsuitable for other reasons. There was Sabrina Guinness, for instance, an acquaintance of Mick Jagger and heiress to an Irish brewery fortune. The social and political ramifications of a union of Charles and Sabrina would have been completely unmanageable.

Some of Charles's relationships were short-lived and casual, such as the one he briefly enjoyed with Laura Jo Watkins, whom the prince met when his ship, the HMS *Jupiter*, docked in California in 1975. There was Jane Ward, who met Charles while working in an office at the Guards Polo Club; Lady Amanda Knatchbull, granddaughter of Lord Mountbatten; and Diana's sister, Lady Sarah Spencer.

The prince had weightier romances with Dale Harper and Camilla Shand, both of whom remained his confidantes after their own marriages. (As we'll see later, Camilla—now Camilla Parker-Bowles—may be far more than merely Charles's confidante.)

The aforementioned Lady Jane Wellesley was just one of a number of close contenders in the "Princess Stakes." Another was Davina Sheffield, who gained the approval of not just the prince, but of his closest relatives and the press, as well. A leggy blonde, she began dating Charles in 1976, after returning from a self-imposed exile to help refugees in Vietnam. Charles's feeling for Davina was real and very deep, but the romance smashed against the rocks when one of her ex-lovers sold his story to the press. It was not much of a story, really, but the mere fact of public acknowledgment that Davina had had a lover at all was enough to ruin her chance to become Princess of Wales.

Another contender was Anna "Whiplash" Wallace. The daughter of a Scottish landowner, Anna came by her nickname thanks to a quick temper and sharp tongue. She was brash and self-confident, shared Charles's passion for hunting, and was completely unawed by the fact that he was Prince of Wales. She treated him as a person, as an equal, and Charles loved it. The match seemed perfect, except

Anna Wallace and Charles shared a deep love of horses. Her nickname "Whiplash," however, referred to her quick temper and independent spirit. She could never get used to Charles's lack of attention and left him after Lord Vestey's ball during which he spent much of the evening dancing with Camilla Parker-Bowles.

for one thing: Anna expected forthright treatment in return, and was prone to raise the roof if she felt she wasn't getting it. When the prince ignored her during the Queen Mother's eightieth birthday party in 1978, Anna stormed angrily from Windsor Castle after warning Charles that "no one treats me like that. Not even you."

Later, at a high society ball in Gloucestershire, Charles ignored Anna again. And to compound the insult, he spent most of the evening dancing with Camilla Parker-Bowles. Anna again left in a huff, putting an end to the saga of Prince Charles and "Whiplash" Wallace.

Diana Spencer remained on the periphery of Charles's life in the late 1970s. In November 1978, a year after her initial meeting with the prince, she was invited, along with sister Sarah, to Buckingham Palace to celebrate Charles's thirtieth birthday. The prince's romance with Sarah had ended by this time, and his date for the evening was actress Susan George. Diana, a year after quitting finishing school, enjoyed herself but certainly entertained no thought that she might someday replace the lissome Ms. George—or any other of the prince's women.

By now living in London, Diana occupied herself mainly with the sort of trivial things that some upper-class young ladies do while waiting for something

Camilla Parker-Bowles has been Charles's friend and confidante for years. Apparently, Diana almost called off the wedding when she found her husband-to-be's gift to Camilla—a gold chain bracelet with a blue enamel disc and the initials "F" and "G" entwined (for "Fred" and "Gladys," their pet names for one another).

important to happen to them. She had lived for three months with family friends in Hampshire, where she cooked, cleaned, and helped look after the couple's six-year-old daughter. The job completed, she had moved to her mother's unoccupied apartment in Belgravia, London, sharing the place with friends Laura Greig and Sophie Kimball. From this home base, Diana took odd jobs with family members and acquaintances.

At 17, Diana was still a quiet girl, more fond of reading and watching television than living the teenage high life. Much of the money she earned from cooking, cleaning (she charged one pound an hour), and cocktail waitressing at private parties went into her bank account.

Finally bored with such undemanding work, Diana took a career step in September 1978 by enrolling in Elizabeth Russell's ten-week cooking course in Wimbledon, southwest London. Her new endeavor had barely begun when her father suffered a near-fatal stroke. The earl's second wife, Raine, kept a bedside vigil and nursed him back to health. He left the hospital in January of 1979, a bit slower than before, a bit slurred in speech, but otherwise fit and happy.

Diana completed her cooking course in the meantime and found easy work as a server with Lumley's,

Lady Tryon (née Dale Harper) was an Australian beauty who met Charles in the late sixties. He affectionately called her "Kanga," in tribute to her national heritage. They parted ways and she married Lord Tryon, but to this day they remain close friends.

After her engagement to Charles, Diana was relentlessly pursued by the press. Always courteous, she never answered a reporter's question with "No comment." As a result, the reporters liked her very much and never gave her a moment's rest.

a catering agency. Still drifting, she left this position and found work as a ballet teacher at a school in south Kensington. For teaching ballet to children aged two to nine, Diana earned £100 a year and had a chance to indulge her own fondness for the art. (At nearly six feet, she was much too tall to seriously consider ballet as a career.)

The ballet job ended when Diana hurt her ankle, so it was back to cooking and cleaning. Help! Then, on her eighteenth birthday on July 1, 1979, she inherited about £60,000 from her American great-grandmother, Fanny Work, whose will had already provided for payouts to older sisters Sarah and Jane. Diana took her mother's advice and invested her windfall in property, a spacious, three-bedroom apartment in a red-brick mansion located in a fashionable area between London's South Kensington and Fulham districts. Diana spent what money remained on apartment rehab and ended up with a very fashionable bachelor-gal pad, which she shared with a revolving set of three girlfriends. Each tenant paid Diana rent of £18 a week, income that Diana supplemented with a child-supervisory job at London's Young England Kindergarten.

Diana's work at the kindergarten filled three afternoons a week. Determined to occupy herself full-time, she went to various employment agencies and found work as a nanny in two different London households.

The net result of all this employment was a dress allowance at Harrods, a Honda Civic (later replaced with a Volkswagen Polo), and a more active social schedule. Diana became a familiar participant in lavish young people's parties held in bars, clubs, and restaurants in exclusive areas of London. Her social circle was expanding, and she was feeling more independent. Although still prone to attacks of shyness, she was certainly far less callow than the 16-year-old Charles had met in 1977.

And what of the prince during the time that Diana was in early flower? Well, to most observers he seemed content to play the field in perpetuity. Although the oldest-ever British bachelor-prince, and al-

With no academic qualifications, taking care of children was one of the few jobs Diana could do as a young woman in London. Even after her marriage, she never stopped working with youngsters. Child-welfare organizations of which she is the patron are delighted.

32

though well aware of his responsibility to eventually select a wife, he did not have a deep craving to take the plunge. Independent of mind and happy when alone, Charles simply did not have a strong emotional need to find a lifelong companion.

It was tragedy that helped push Charles to the altar. On August 27, 1979, Lord Mountbatten and three companions were killed in a fishing-boat explosion off the Irish coast; three days later, two members of the Irish Republican Army were accused of murdering the 79-year-old Mountbatten, a hero of World War II and Charles's great-uncle and mentor. Not long before his death, "Uncle Dickie" had urged Charles to think seriously about a bride. Now, with Mountbatten gone, the fire was finally lit beneath the prince.

Word leaked out that the search was on, and the press went wild. Amidst all the hubbub, Charles diligently prepared his resources of energy and judgment, in order to make the right choice.

Like planets that silently fall into the same orbit, Charles and Diana once again came together. In January 1979, Diana had been invited by the queen to join family and friends at Sandringham for a shooting weekend. The invitation happened because of elder sister Jane, by then married to the queen's assistant private secretary, Robert Fellowes.

Then, in February of 1980, Diana was in the party that went to see Charles play polo with his team, Les Diables Bleus (Blue Devils), at Cowdray Park in Midhurst, Sussex. Soon after, at the Duke of Richmond's Goodwood House Ball, thrown to mark the conclusion of the Royal Goodwood horse race week, guests could not help but notice how closely Charles and Diana danced.

This was followed by the prince's invitation to have Diana accompany him to a performance of Verdi's *Requiem* at London's Royal Albert Hall. Although Diana's grandmother, Lady Ruth Fermoy, came along to chaperone, the air seemed charged with romance.

In August 1980, Diana joined the royal family aboard their yacht, *Britannia*, for a cruise. She took full advantage of an interlude of windsurfing to show off her shapely figure within view of the prince, and even to tip over the mast of his Windsurfer. Although drenched, Charles apparently maintained a happy frame of mind, for Diana was once again in his company a month later at Balmoral.

One of Charles's main interests before his marriage was polo. He is considered to be one of the best polo players in England. The prince still continues to play the game, even though it does not hold much interest for his wife.

By now it was obvious to people inside the royal family and to a few sharp observers on the outside that Charles was developing strong feelings for Lady Diana Spencer. The press finally got wind of the romance when reporters spied Charles and Diana fishing for salmon in the River Dee at Balmoral.

As ever, the British tabloids were the antithesis of restraint. "HE'S IN LOVE AGAIN!" was the headline that leaped from the front page of the September 8, 1980, edition of *The Sun*. A hardly more respectful subhead declared, "Lady Di is the new girl for Charles."

Lady Di was also the new girl for the Fleet Street press establishment, whose members were delighted to discover that her apartment was close to the kindergarten where she worked. Thus, a veritable herd of paparazzi was parked outside Diana's digs at all hours of the day and night. For a while, Diana was able to elude the professional snoops by entering and exiting the main mansion through a service door. If she dared to get into her car to venture into the street, cars full of reporters would often follow her;

Before the wedding, Diana joined Prince Andrew (left) and her fiancé (right) at a polo match in Windsor. The future princess learned all too soon that royal life involved many social obligations that were not necessarily very interesting to her.

Diana got lost in traffic more than once while trying to elude her pursuers.

Occasionally, though, the last laugh was Diana's, as when she piqued the interest of the gathered press vultures by soberly loading an overnight bag into her car, then walking to a nearby shop. While the reporters waited for her to return to the loaded car, Diana got beyond their line of sight and made her escape. The hapless reporters did not see her again until days later, when she returned from a relaxed weekend at Althorp.

But even the most cunning game of hide-and-seek becomes wearying if carried on too long. After weeks of unrelenting pressure from the press, Diana began to wobble. Her mother fired an angry letter to *The Times*: "May I ask the editors of Fleet Street, whether, in the execution of their jobs, they consider it necessary or fair to harass my daughter daily, from dawn until well after dusk? Is it fair to ask any human being, regardless of circumstances, to be treated in this way?"

Freedom of the press was one thing, Frances asserted; gross intrusion quite another.

For Diana, not yet 20 years old, the intense scrutiny and media hype were almost too much to bear. Still a girl in a woman's body, she was being swept along on a tide of frighteningly powerful emotions. If things developed as the press had speculated, she wanted to have the presence of mind necessary for a proper decision.

Charles, too, had serious thinking to do. Although by now almost inured to the shenanigans of the press establishment, he nevertheless had to look objectively at Diana, at himself, and at his responsibility to Britain. He had been enchanted by Diana's beauty, vivacity, and innate sweetness. On the other hand, if he married her, she would be thrust into a terribly demanding role for which she had had no training or preparation. Charles consulted with aides, asked the opinion of confidantes, and spent long hours in solitary thought.

Finally, on February 6, 1981, after returning from his annual ski holiday to Klosters, Charles, Prince of Wales, took Lady Diana Spencer into the nursery at Windsor Castle and proposed marriage. Diana accepted. Charles notified Queen Elizabeth by phone, and Diana told her parents and siblings the next day. The momentous news was released to the world on February 24.

What manner of cynic would have dared to suggest that the pair would not live happily ever after?

Becoming a princess involved many photo opportunities, as Diana quickly learned. Luckily, the young lady was very attractive and photogenic. Soon girls all over the country tried to copy her clothes, her hair, and her regal look.

The strapless black dress that Diana wore to the royal couple's first formal evening engagement together at the Goldsmith's Hall created quite a stir. Some sources say the queen was not pleased with the dress's gravity-defying neckline and its black color.

The Wedding of the Century .... and the Morning After

When Diana stared into the central oval sapphire of her magnificent, £28,500 engagement ring, she looked not merely at a splendid stone that was surrounded by 14 diamonds set in white gold; she looked at a symbol of the glory that had been Britain.

She, too, had become a symbol. She was going to be a princess. Indisputably, her life had been changed, completely and forever. She had become part of a long-standing tradition, a fact that was symbolized by the royal family's gift to her of the late Queen Mary's diamond and emerald pendant.

With the official announcement that Charles would wed Lady Diana Spencer at St. Paul's Cathedral on July 29, 1981, Diana was given over to the people of Britain, and the world. Henceforth, she would no longer be a private person but a creature who belonged to Britain and the public. Crowds gathered outside her apartment immediately after the announcement, unaware that she had left it behind for good. Until the wedding, her residence would be at Clarence House, where she would be attended to by her grandmother, Lady Ruth Fermoy, and by Charles's grandmother, the Queen Mother.

The wedding of Lady Diana Spencer and Charles, Prince of Wales, took place on July 29, 1981, at St. Paul's Cathedral in London. Opposite: The bride walked the aisle accompanied by her father, the 8th Earl Spencer.

In the meantime, there was much to do. It was Charles himself who selected St. Paul's Cathedral as the wedding venue, instead of the traditional Westminster Abbey. For years, Charles had been enamored of the idea of a musical wedding, so the cathedral's superior acoustics made it an obvious choice. He and Diana would walk up the aisle to music by Purcell, Handel, and Jeremiah Clarke; following the ceremony, they would retrace their steps to the strains of Edward Elgar and Sir William Walton. The music would be played by the assembled talents of three orchestras, together with the Bach Choir and the sublimely talented New Zealand opera diva, Kiri Te Kanawa.

Because of the British monarchy's close ties to the world of religion, the couple's choice of wedding hymns was highly significant. Charles selected "Christ Is Made the Sure Foundation"; Diana chose "I Vow to Thee My Country."

Beautiful in casual dress, Diana promised to be a ravishing bride. She selected David and Elizabeth Emanuel to design her gown, a stunning creation in ivory-colored English silk embroidered with pearls and mother-of-pearl sequins. Extensive frills of lace

36

The bridal party consisted of (from left to right): Edward van Cutsem, Catherine Cameron, Lord Nicholas Windsor, India Hicks, Sarah Jane Gasalee, Prince Edward, Charles and Diana, Prince Andrew, Lady Sarah Armstrong-Jones, and Clementine Hambro.

complemented ruffled sleeves and a V-shaped neckline and bodice. The veil was made of fine silk and decorated with mother-of-pearl sequins.

In line with bridal tradition, Diana would wear "something old" (the lace, which had belonged to Queen Mary), "something borrowed" (her mother's earrings), and "something blue" (a small bow sewn onto the waist of her gown, and complemented with a tiny gold horseshoe).

Diana's five bridesmaids would wear more subdued ivory dresses, while the two pageboys would wear Royal Navy cadet uniforms that dated back to 1863, the year of the last state wedding of a Prince of Wales, when the future King Edward VII married Alexandra of Denmark.

Charles would be married while wearing his Royal Navy commander's uniform.

As Diana's gown was being fitted and altered, the princess-to-be had to endure endless practicing of the bridal walk, the subtle royal hand-wave, and the appropriately benign gaze that the Princess of Wales should offer to her subjects. This was demanding, physical work that became particularly difficult when compounded by the frenzied attention of the press and electronic media. Cameras never stopped click-

ing during Diana's public appearances. She had to put across a particularly serene, attractive image while doing an engagement interview on television with Charles; her awareness that her face and remarks were being absorbed by a worldwide audience of some 700 million people must have been overwhelming.

Finally, the pressure became too great to bear: While watching Charles play polo at Tidworth in Wiltshire, Diana openly burst into tears and had to be helped into her car by her fiancé.

Preparations for the wedding continued. Two thousand, six hundred and fifty wedding invitations had been mailed out by Lord Chamberlain, the person responsible for the overall planning of the event. Gifts, letters, and postcards arrived from around the world—the congratulations of presidents and

Before the happy couple left St. Paul's Cathedral, they signed wedding register Number 345. It showed that "Charles P." (Princeps, Latin for prince) had married "Diana Spencer, spinster."

The 25-foot-long train and veil were so difficult to maneuver that Diana spent countless hours before the wedding getting into and out of the glass carriage.

schoolchildren, sheikhs and housewives. In all, the royal couple received 100,000 letters and more than 3,000 gifts.

On the night of July 28, the day before the wedding, Charles visited Hyde Park to ignite the first of 101 bonfires that would coincide with similar celebrations throughout the nation. Half a million people crowded the park, bringing an electric enthusiasm that was matched across Britain.

Earlier that evening, Diana did another television interview, in which she said she looked forward to her wedding and her new role. She praised Charles as "a tower of strength." By the time her fiancé lit the first bonfire, she was already preparing for bed, and the momentous day that would begin at 6:30 the following morning.

At 10:37 A.M. on July 29, the horse-drawn glass coach that carried Diana and her father embarked on its journey from Clarence House to St. Paul's, where Charles and the royal family waited with other heads of state, sports and entertainment celebrities, friends of the bride and groom, and more than 200

members of the staffs from Buckingham Palace, Windsor Castle, Sandringham, and Balmoral.

Johnnie Spencer, left with a slight limp from his stroke but otherwise hale, accompanied his daughter up the aisle to the altar.

The ceremony lasted 70 minutes. Diana's wedding ring had been carved from the same nugget of Welsh gold as that used to make wedding rings for the Queen Mother, Queen Elizabeth II, Princess Margaret, and Princess Anne. As the Archbishop of Canterbury, Robert Runcie, pronounced the couple man and wife, a huge cheer shook the interior of the cathedral. Outside, 600,000 people who had been listening to the ceremony over speakers sent up a cry of their own.

Shortly afterward, when the entire royal family stood on a balcony of Buckingham Palace, the Prince and new Princess of Wales kissed each other on the lips, a break with royal tradition that was enthusiastically received by the gathered throng below.

Following the snapping of the official wedding portraits (taken with five synchronized cameras), the 118 dinner guests partook of a three-course meal of brill in lobster sauce, "supreme de volaille Princesse de Galles," and strawberries and cream. The hexagonal wedding cake was five feet high, with five tiers and a weight of 255 pounds. It was cut by Charles with his ceremonial sword.

After dinner, the newlyweds changed into comfortable clothes and left by carriage for Waterloo Station, smiling and waving at the crowds that lined the route. Next came a ride on the royal train to Broadlands, the Hampshire home of Lord and Lady Romsey, and the former residence of Lord Mountbatten. Princess Elizabeth and Prince Philip had spent their wedding night at the house in 1947.

Charles and Diana relaxed at Broadlands for a couple days, then flew (with Charles at the controls) to Gibraltar, where, on the last day of July, they boarded the royal yacht *Britannia* for a Mediterranean cruise. Snorkeling, scuba diving, sunbathing, and beach barbecues would fill their days and evenings.

Diana and Charles returned to the United Kingdom in mid-August, touching down in a Royal Air Force VC.10 in Scotland, intending to join the royal

After dinner and a change into comfortable clothes, Diana and Charles took a carriage to Waterloo Station to catch a train to Broadlands, the first stop of the royal honeymoon. They smiled and waved to well-wishers lining the route.

family at Balmoral. Over the past half-month, Diana had become more confident, and readied herself for another interlude of relaxation.

What she found at Balmoral, though, was boredom. Charles loved the 24,000-acre estate and enjoyed fishing and just rambling about, often by himself or with cronies from his bachelor days. Diana wanted desperately to talk to her new husband, to learn about him, to talk about their future life together. This was not to be, and if Diana was upset about it, Charles could only wonder why. What did she expect? She had never complained about being at Balmoral before—why start now?

The queen's suggestion to Diana that she invite some favorite girlfriends to the estate brightened the princess's demeanor somewhat, but only temporarily. She found most of her time at Balmoral unrewarding and stultifying.

The newlyweds returned to London in late autumn and took up residence in their apartment inside Buckingham Palace. On November 5, 1981, it was officially announced that the Princess of Wales would give birth to a baby the following June. Millions of people around the globe were cheered by the news. For Diana, it meant severe morning sickness and a daily struggle to perform her duties. Regardless, on her first official visit to Wales in late October, she charmed the people there with her shyness and fresh good looks. She made her first public speech, most of it in Welsh, saying "How proud I am to be Princess of such a wonderful place, and the Welsh, who are very special to me."

Not everyone in Wales was thrilled by Diana's presence. Nationalist sentiment dates back to the

Standing on the balcony of Buckingham Palace with the wedding party and royal family, Prince Charles kissed the new Princess Diana on the lips. This break with tradition was an enormous crowd-pleaser.

When a honeymoon is as long as Charles's and Diana's (three months), there is time for a variety of activities. The royal honeymooners attended the Braemar Highland Games at Balmoral, where the crowds admired the princess's Scottish plaid suit and jaunty black tam-o'-shanter.

13th century, when the invading King Edward I killed the last Welsh prince and installed his own son as Prince of Wales. The succession has continued ever since, raising the ire of some Welsh citizens and inspiring a tradition of threats against the British monarchy. Security precautions, then, were one more reality with which Diana had to contend.

In the main, though, the beautiful princess was acclaimed across Wales. Charles accepted his relegation to "second-class" status with good humor; he had been in the spotlight his entire life, and was willing—at least for the time being—to witness most of the attention going to his bride.

By the close of 1981, Diana was beginning to become distressed by the constant press attention. A "truce" that was arranged by the palace with the editors of Britain's legitimate newspapers was blithely ignored by the tabloids, which continued to bore in fiercely on Diana. The tabloids' zeal became painfully apparent in February of 1982, when a pair of photographers armed with high-power zoom lenses hacked their way through a Bahamanian jungle to take pictures of the bikini-clad, pregnant princess, who was innocently vacationing with her husband. Buckingham Palace pronounced the invasion "taste-

less"—small comfort to Diana, who had to cope not just with the press, but with a marriage that was already in trouble.

Diana's mood brightened, of course, when the couple's first child, Prince William, was born on June 21, 1982, ten days short of Diana's twenty-first birthday. But the familiar routine soon reasserted itself, and the blue funk once again descended over the apartment in Buckingham Palace. Essentially, it had become clear that Diana and Charles had little in common. Many of the prince's favorite activities, which Diana had been willing to share during the courtship, now held no interest for her. Charles felt as though he had been duped, while Diana was convinced that he was simply stubborn, unwilling to bend a bit and do something that she might like. At the very least, couldn't he just *talk* to her?

It was an impasse. Charles wondered if Diana weren't a bit empty-headed; Diana was becoming convinced that Charles was cold and arrogant.

Diana got engaged, married, and pregnant all within the space of nine months. During that time, she surpassed all of the members of the royal family in popularity polls.

Worse, he was determined to see people from his past, old flames included. Dale Harper, an Australian who later moved to England and married Lord Tryon, was one; Charles affectionately called her Kanga. With her husband in tow, she was a frequent visitor to the royal residences.

Another, more threatening old flame was Camilla Parker-Bowles, the former Camilla Shand and niece of Lord Ashcombe, whom Charles had met when both were in their early twenties. Although seriously in love with her at the time, young Charles had simply been unwilling to make a marriage commitment. But because they shared many interests and keenly understood each other, they remained close friends. Indeed, Camilla is known throughout Britain as Charles's "chief confidante."

Diana didn't like it. She viewed Kanga and especially Camilla as threats, and shuddered to think what her husband was confiding to them that he was not sharing with her. Even more off-putting to Diana was the thought that Charles had long used Camilla to help him pass judgment on his girlfriends. What on earth might Camilla have said about Diana? The

princess hardly wanted to consider it, but she was compelled to. Doubt and fear built up inside her.

Diana was feeling increasingly isolated, and not just because of the clash of her busy schedule with Charles's. The truth was that, intellectually and personally, she and Charles were worlds apart.

In many ways a typical male member of his class, the prince enjoyed gathering with like-minded friends to indulge in the familiar catalog of upper-crust pursuits: pot shots at fox and grouse, a bit of fishing, plenty of polo. Diana endured the endless polo matches as a spectator but had an aversion to any sort of blood sport, despite having been raised in an atmosphere that relished such pastimes.

The list of conflicts between Diana and Charles did not end with their differing notions of sport. Classical music and serious drama occupied a significant portion of Charles's leisure time, while Diana favored pop music and TV soap operas. Charles absorbed serious, weighty novels while Diana preferred to read romance novels and fashion magazines. The country life held enormous appeal for Charles; Diana preferred life in town. His idea of a perfect vacation was a ski holiday in Switzerland; hers was to lie by the swimming pool and soak up the sun. Compared to these differences, the 13 years that separated them seemed inconsequential.

As the couple grew further apart, Diana interpreted the situation as a lack of love on Charles's part. Although desperate for his approval, she seemed unable—or perhaps unwilling—to give him what he wanted.

Diana and Charles named their first son William Arthur Philip Louis according to the royal custom of giving a child names held by previous royals. The christening was held on the Queen Mother's eighty-second birthday on August 4, 1982.

Diana, Charles, and baby William went to live in the newly decorated apartments at Kensington Palace. Determined to spend as much time as possible with his son, Charles initially cut down on his royal engagements. Many were critical of him for this decision.

Charles, too, may have been stubborn, unwilling to follow the give-and-take course that defines successful marriages. He spent increasing amounts of time at his own pursuits, leaving Diana alone, emotionally adrift. Loneliness soon came to characterize the princess's life.

If the pair's private life soon became a shambles, their public life was hardly better. Their spats often became apparent to outsiders, and public appearances that were designed to showcase both Charles and Diana began to go awry. One evening in 1982, the couple was expected to attend the annual Festival of Remembrance at Royal Albert Hall in London, in honor of Britain's war dead. When the big evening arrived, Diana announced that because she had spent the past few nights sleeplessly attending to baby William, she was too tired to attend. Charles insisted that Diana change her mind. She refused. The prince, convinced that his duty took precedence over his loyalty to his wife, stormed from the room.

This sort of blow-up would have been bad enough if the incident had ended there, but Charles took additional offense when Diana arrived at the Festival anyway—15 minutes late and unannounced, after Charles had informed the press that she would not be present, and after workers acting on the prince's orders had removed her seat from the royal box at Albert Hall. The moment was not simply awkward but embarrassing, for royal protocol dictates that the monarch arrive at public functions *after* everyone else—family included.

The Albert Hall incident is just one of many that can be cited in the early course of the royal marriage. Not surprisingly, the tabloid press seized upon it

and similar unhappy incidents with undisguised glee, trumpeting every squabble, every public huff and spat in enormous black headlines and with melodramatic photographs. Unauthorized bikini images are graceless, but many of the tabloid photos are even more disturbing—heartbreaking telephoto shots of the unhappy Diana: her eyes filled with tears; her head bowed; her hand held to her face in an ineffectual attempt to hide her misery. The public has been simultaneously fascinated and repelled by such images. Never before had a failing royal marriage been laid bare for all to see.

Valentine's Day, 1984, brought the official announcement that the princess was pregnant once again. As before, Diana suffered fearsome morning sickness, a situation that surely did not improve her general frame of mind.

Prince Henry Charles Albert David—affectionately known as Harry—was born on September 15, 1984. Although Charles cut back on his public activities in order to spend more time with Diana and the children, he began to insist that William, by now an active and demanding child, be better restrained by his mother. Discipline had played an important part in Charles's own upbringing, and he expected the same attitude to be instilled in his successor.

The biggest break arose over the question of boarding school. Diana did not want the boys to be sent away at age eight, as had been the case with herself and Charles. Instead, she wanted to keep them at home until at least the age of 12. Charles would have none of this notion and pulled rank on Diana, in-

New mother Diana was very happy to spend as much time as possible with her baby and husband. Soon, however, their marriage relationship began to deteriorate as the princess refused to take her royal duties as seriously as members of the family wished her to.

sisting that each boy would go to Ludgrove School in Berkshire at age eight.

Of all the painful lessons Diana has learned since her marriage, the one that looms largest of all is that royal tradition cannot be changed, and perhaps not even bent, by a newcomer. Charles, too, faces a hard truth: His mother is disinclined to step down and allow him to assume the job for which he has spent his entire life rehearsing and being trained. Each of the marriage partners, then, is frustrated, stonewalled.

A 45-minute interview with the couple that ran on Britain's Independent Television Network in 1985 (it aired in shorter form in America on ABC-TV's *20/20*) presented a relaxed (and well-coached) royal couple. The interview was granted in an attempt to quash rumors about the couple's unhappiness, but real-life events gave lie to the whole effort. During a tour of Vienna, for example, Diana became visibly angry with the flirtatious wife of the city's mayor; in Vancouver, Canada, where the couple opened Expo '86, Diana fainted and slumped into her husband's arms; during a subsequent tour of Japan, Diana was ill-tempered with photographers.

According to Lady Colin Campbell's book, *Diana in Private*, it was at about this time that Charles resurrected his relationship with Camilla Parker-Bowles. Diana became furious, but her anger only drove Charles farther away. To console herself, Diana consorted with Sarah Ferguson, the vivacious daughter of Charles's polo manager, Major Ronald Ferguson. Windblown and casual, "Fergie" provided Diana with a welcome antidote to the stuffiness of Charles and castle life. Because of her friendship with Diana, Fergie eventually came into the orbit of Prince Andrew, whom she married in July of 1986. Once installed as the Duchess of York, Fergie was free to devote even more time to Diana's "liberation," introducing the princess to her own set of younger, socially uninhibited friends, and encouraging Diana's innate love of pranks and mischief. (Cameras clicked madly when the Princess and the Duchess poked society girl Lulu Blacker and Major Hugh Lindsay, a friend of Charles, in the backsides with umbrellas during a day at Ascot in June 1987!)

Nightclubbing, party-going, and even party-*crashing* soon came to define the activities of Diana and Sarah, whom the press dubbed the "Throne Rangers." The newsies were particularly intrigued by Diana's highly visible friendship with Philip Dunne,

Weatherly School is the destination for the uniform-clad Princes Harry and William. Diana is the type of mother who likes to be very involved with her sons' upbringing. She often takes them to school and picks them up herself.

the grandson of Princess Alexandra. Dunne became a familiar figure at Charles and Diana's ski vacations, and later enjoyed Diana's attentions at a wedding party at Ascot; as the pair danced together, Diana ran her fingers through Dunne's hair and kissed him on the cheek, in full view of the assembled guests. Did Charles notice? Well, no, because he was in deep conversation with Camilla Parker-Bowles! He left the party alone at 2:00 A.M.

The marriage of Sarah Ferguson and Prince Andrew had a liberating effect on Diana. Fergie introduced the princess to her younger friends and the two of them had a lot of carefree fun together. Unfortunately, marriage has not worked out for the Duke and Duchess of York.

Predictably, Charles found that he had very little in common with his wife's new friends. Most of the people in his own circle were reserved and bookish —although that does not adequately explain the presence in his life of Camilla or of socialites the likes of the Marchesa di Frescobaldi, Patti Palmer-Tompkinson, Candida Lycett-Green, Lady Sarah Keswick, and Eva O'Neill. Like Diana, Charles looked for consolation in the company of others.

Press reports claimed that the royal couple spent their sixth wedding anniversary apart. Three months later, in October 1987, they came together to greet flood victims in Wales. They had not seen each other at that point for a month, yet their behavior toward each other was aloof, even icy. As soon as the appearance was over, Charles flew back to Balmoral, where Camilla was a secret house guest.

Ironically, Diana seemed most disturbed by the fact that her friend Fergie was gathering an awful lot of media attention, and was edging the princess from the limelight. Diana's ego was bruised, and she decided to do something about it. After a visit to the Arab Gulf States in November 1987, she allegedly claimed that the Arabs had gone "ga-ga" at the sight of her. In February of the following year, during a trip to Portugal, Diana openly flirted with the country's 62-year-old president, Dr. Mario Soares, topping off her performance with the question, "If I get cold, will you warm me up?"

Clearly, Diana was making an effort to push Fergie off the front pages. But were there other motives behind her behavior? Did she hope to make Charles jealous? Was she intent merely on taking revenge on him? Or was it just a way to demonstrate her independence?

Whatever the reason, Diana soon discovered that her behavior benefited nobody except the members of the press. The queen, not unjustifiably, was upset with her daughter-in-law's carryings-on, particularly because it cast Charles and the throne in a bad light. Whether or not Elizabeth sat down with the couple and told them to behave, at least when in public, is unknown, but it is a fact that the palace contacted Philip Dunne and instructed him to stop seeing the Princess of Wales.

Dunne receded into the background, but Diana found a replacement in the person of Captain James Hewitt, a member of the Life Guards who first met Diana to give her and the boys lessons in horsemanship. Diana appreciated Hewitt's straightforward manner and sense of fun, and she and the boys spent considerable, happy weekends with him and his parents at the Hewitt home in Devon. In time, the palace sent Hewitt essentially the same message it sent to Philip Dunne, and his relationship with Diana cooled.

The princess was shocked from her absorption in her own situation in March of 1988, when Charles was nearly killed by an avalanche that swept through a ski party at Klosters. Charles's close friend, Major Hugh Lindsay, died beneath the roaring snow, leaving the prince in a state of shock and Diana hurrying to his side. She provided Charles with the anchor he needed in order to deal with the tragedy, and kept a cool head when others momentarily lost theirs. It was a terrible interlude that nevertheless allowed Diana to look at herself in a new way; she could feel her self-confidence returning.

Although no official celebration was arranged to mark Diana's thirtieth birthday on July 1, 1991 (Charles's camp informed the press that the prince had offered his wife a celebration but that she had

An informal portrait taken amid the wildflowers of Highgrove shows a five-year-old Prince William and a three-year-old Prince Harry with their parents. Although Diana prefers life in London, she welcomes the escape to the country some weekends.

Official duties take Diana to all corners of the globe. On her trip to Egypt, she had the opportunity to visit many interesting sites. She is an excellent ambassador for Britain, since people all over the world seem drawn to her smile and friendly manner.

turned the idea down), the couple's subsequent public appearances were reasonably upbeat. They seemed friendly, even affectionate. The death of Diana's father on March 29, 1992, was a devastating blow, of course, but the couple managed to present a united front to the media.

The pair's separate vacations that followed the earl's funeral provoked some press comment, but the explosion came in June, when pre-publicity for *Diana: Her True Story,* a book written by ex-tabloid reporter Andrew Morton, alleged that Diana had nearly called off her wedding to Charles after discovering a gold chain bracelet that Charles insisted on giving to Camilla Parker-Bowles. The bracelet had a blue enamel disc with the entwined letters "F" and "G," standing for Fred and Gladys, Charles and Camilla's pet names for each other.

Morton further claimed that while on her honeymoon Diana noticed her husband was wearing cufflinks in the shape of two intertwined letter "C"s—Camilla and Charles. Morton claimed that the cufflinks had been a gift from Camilla.

The book also painted Diana as a compulsive bulimic whose existence was defined by eating binges and self-induced, purgative vomiting.

Morton's most shocking assertion was that Diana had attempted suicide five times. Allegedly, she had cut her wrists with a razor blade; thrown herself against a glass cabinet at Kensington Palace; stabbed herself in the chest and thighs with a penknife; cut herself with the serrated edge of a lemon slicer; and hurled herself down a full flight of stairs at Sandringham House when three months pregnant with Prince William.

Although not life-threatening suicide attempts, these incidents, if true, may certainly be viewed as pathetic cries for help from a profoundly unhappy person. Morton claimed that much of his information came from Diana's closest friends, many of whom would never say a word about her without first getting her permission.

For her part, Camilla Parker-Bowles, referred to by the Diana of Morton's book as "the Rottweiler,"

Royal duties can sometimes take Diana to the most unlikely places. During her tour of the Tidworth Royal Hampshire Regiment, the princess got a firsthand look at the inside of a tank.

professed unconcern. "I'm certainly not going to bury myself away because of what the papers say," she told a group of reporters after she and her husband shared tea with the queen. "Absolutely not. Why should I?"

The book flew off store shelves when it became available. Readers, as well as people who had not yet seen a copy, debated it endlessly. The palace responded by going on the offensive, encouraging Charles and Diana not only to accelerate their schedule of public appearances, but to make appearances *together*.

On June 21, the two of them dressed in cowboy costumes and appeared to have fun at a North London party for Prince William's tenth birthday, and the ninth birthday of Theodora, the daughter of the party's host, ex-King Constantine of Greece.

The conflicting tone of the couple's public appearances and the horrors described in Morton's book did little to bring the full picture into focus. In the absence of irrefutable facts, self-styled experts

Diana took the 1992 death of her father, the 8th Earl Spencer, very hard. She attended his funeral at St. Mary the Virgin Church in Great Brighton with members of her family.

popped up to throw in their two cents. One of these was Maya Parker, a leading Harley Street, London, therapist who, as inelegantly described by the *Today* newspaper, had "counseled countless famous clients with similar problems to Diana's." Parker asserted that the only person who could relieve Diana's problems was Diana herself. The therapist claimed that because of Diana's disrupted childhood, she had never grown up. She was like "a naughty teenager, and whatever her sweet public image, she can be a very nasty one, too. . . . she must seek the right kind of help."

One Stephen Twigg, who was reportedly visiting the princess at least once a week to impart "psychological counseling and massage," urged Charles and the rest of the royal family to take immediate steps to alleviate Diana's emotional distress. Without that sort of intervention, Diana would deteriorate rapidly. "The situation has to end," Twigg warned, "or there will be a tragedy."

Outsiders' views aside, if Diana did use Morton's book as a sly way to publicly air her grievances, the act can be perceived as one of strong will as easily as one of childish weakness. The princess's past behavior suggests that her character contains both of those dimensions, so either rationale is possible. Whatever the truth of her involvement in Morton's book, though, one conclusion seems inescapable: Although cast in a real-life fairy tale, Diana has discovered that someone forgot to give her the part of the script with the happy ending.

Charity work is one of the princess's favorite endeavors. Her own unhappiness has made her extremely sympathetic to the needs and problems of those less fortunate.

The Royal Routine

At least part of Diana's general unhappiness has undoubtedly arisen from the rigid structure of her days—days that do not really belong to her, but that are planned for her by others. Her official obligations are many. Although she occasionally has lunch with members of her staff and even allows her favorites to call her by her first name, she remains the Princess of Wales; the royal routine

The young royals' apartments at Kensington Palace, or KP as it is affectionately called, are large, bright, and airy, with massive windows. The princess had them newly decorated with the help of Diana and Dudley Poplak.

and protocol that define most of Diana's existence are not taken lightly by the royal family. Indeed, Diana's life is severely proscribed, her every move scheduled, preplanned, and closely observed by her protectors. There's a lot of truth in the old cliché about life in a goldfish bowl. Diana has learned during the years of her marriage that Kensington Palace, Buckingham Palace, and the other royal residences may be the most wearying goldfish bowls around.

The life of most people is a reasonably agreeable mix of routine and spontaneity. We have things that we must do at about the same times every day, but we also have the freedom to inject a bit of caprice into our lives; on particularly daring days, we can chuck the daily routine altogether and do as we please. Not so for Diana, whose schedule is carefully planned a full six months in advance, and who can throw an enormous staff and untold numbers of

strangers into a tizzy if she decides she wants to make a change in that schedule.

Diana was barely out of her teens when she entered the world of royal protocol and security. She had to become accustomed not only to a sobering set of responsibilities, but to working with an enormous staff that included cooks, a hairdresser, a butler, a lady-in-waiting, a private secretary, nannies, and a virtual army of bodyguards and security experts. And, oh yes, she also had to accustom herself to dealing with that fellow named Charles.

Ironically, the course of the royal routine often carries Diana and her husband in completely different directions. When under the same roof, they rise separately, dress separately, breakfast separately, and look at their newspapers and private mail separately. Once ready to face the world, they usually do not face it together. Clearly, Diana's marriage is as much a job as it is a relationship.

Job or not, Diana refuses to be an automaton, a wind-up toy. Although she takes her official responsibilities seriously, she is most serious about being a good mother. Daily normalcy is important

Although Princess Diana likes shopping, it is never a spontaneous activity, as it often is for the rest of us. Stores are notified of her impending arrival and security is always tight.

One of Diana's goals is to give her boys as much of a normal childhood as possible. Since all children love to play, they are encouraged to do so as much as they like when they are on vacation at Highgrove.

to her, particularly as it relates to the rearing of her sons, William and Harry. Unlike many previous royal mothers, Diana tends to many of her children's needs herself, preferring not to let the boys' nannies take over every motherly function. When away from the boys, Diana carries photographs of them and stays in close touch by telephone.

Essentially easygoing, Diana strives to create a relaxed, loving environment for the "heir and spare," and sees to it that both boys have ample opportunities to play and behave as much as possible like ordinary children. Charles is of the opinion that the boys have too much freedom and not nearly enough discipline, and he may be right. William, a scrappy lad known around his school as "Bill the Basher," is given to temper tantrums and the occasional "wait-until-I'm-king" sort of self-assertion. The boy raised his mother's ire in memorable fashion during School Sports Day in Richmond Park in 1990, when he found himself turned over Diana's knee and publicly spanked for disobedience. (Predictably, the tabloids thought Diana's performance was completely uncalled for.)

Diana reasons that exposure to a spectrum of life removed from the narrow, rather artificial confines of the royal family will be good for the boys. She may have had her finest moment as a mother when she

decided to introduce William and Harry to her friend, Adrian Ward-Jackson, who was dying of AIDS. Human suffering can be tempered by loving gestures, and Diana wanted her sons to witness both.

All of Britain suffered a nasty scare in June 1991, when William suffered a depressed fracture of the skull after being accidentally rapped by a golf club at school. Diana was at his side as doctors at the Royal Berkshire hospital tested and examined him. Later, she rode with him in the ambulance as he was sped to surgery at London's Great Ormond Street Hospital for Sick Children.

Diana's behavior during this crisis only endeared her more to her subjects, but Charles did himself no good at all by deciding to continue his normal schedule after hearing about the accident. As his son was being operated on, Charles was entertaining European Community officials at a Covent Garden performance of *Tosca*; while William recuperated the next day, Charles attended an environmental conference in North Yorkshire. The *Sun*'s headline, "What kind of dad are you?," practically screamed off the page.

William's accident turned up the excitement level of Diana's life by more than a few notches. On typical days, though, her routine is predictable and unsurprising. When the princess stays in London at Kensington Palace, for instance, her days are ordered and precise. Kensington Palace—often called KP—was built by Sir Christopher Wren and is the birthplace of Queen Victoria and Queen Mary. Charles and Diana live in apartments 8 and 9; other palace residents include Prince and Princess Michael of Kent, and Princess Margaret.

"Apartment" may be a misleading word, for the palace is enormous and so are the individual living units. Expansive, stately, and well patrolled by security men, KP does not have the cozy sort of layout that encourages neighborly drop-ins for muffins and tea. But even with the palace's considerable space, Charles and Diana have felt compelled to move their offices a couple of miles away, to St. James's Palace.

When William and Harry are staying at Kensington Palace, separate, self-contained bedroom suites are provided for them. Each suite comes complete with kitchen, bathroom, and staff bedrooms.

Diana's activities while she lives at KP follow a schedule that is typed and distributed to her staff at the beginning of each week. Preparations are made accordingly. Each day begins before 8:30 A.M., when

Nanny Barbara Barnes accompanied Diana, Charles, and William on their trip to Australia and New Zealand in 1983. Later, she was dismissed as royal nanny for reasons that are not entirely clear.

The royal life of propriety and protocol can be a difficult one to endure on an everyday basis. Sometimes even a beautiful princess needs to dress up in ordinary clothes and go for a walk by herself.

Diana rises and greets her personal dresser, who has already laid out the princess's jewelry and wardrobe.

Diana's hairdresser arrives at the dressing room adjacent to Diana's bedroom at 8:30 and works his magic. Makeup is also applied, and then it's time for breakfast, which usually consists of grapefruit, cereal, yogurt, and Earl Grey tea with lemon. Diana's glance at the newspapers (tabloids excluded, one supposes) and mail marks the end of the morning.

What happens next varies, of course, but on the days Diana is scheduled to go shopping on Kensington High Street, for example, Scotland Yard and the London Ambulance Service are informed in advance. When Diana is driven from the south entrance of Kensington Palace, her bodyguard and his high-frequency radio are her close companions. The police track her movements by computer, and an ambulance will be waiting at each of her destinations, ready if needed. If the jaunt is far enough to require a helicopter, the copter's progress is monitored through binoculars and radio by a fire brigade officer stationed on a rooftop.

Although Diana hates horses and riding, Prince William learned to ride at a very early age. His riding style is very correct and stylish, and he loves to jump over hedges and fences.

Even something as simple as lunch at a restaurant means that Diana will be surrounded by more than 20 people involved in her upkeep and security. They follow her everywhere—when she shops, eats, plays tennis, and visits with her family and friends.

In the main, Diana gets on well with her staff members, but there have been stories that suggest all is not smooth sailing. Although the princess has admitted to being a perfectionist, she has also claimed to be a fair employer. "I just don't sack people," she told *Daily Mirror* royal correspondent James Whitaker in 1985. Well, she might not sack them directly, but she can certainly ignore them until they resign, or find someone else to do the firing for her. Insiders have alleged that the princess can be the model of kindness one moment and irascible the next. A recent victim of her wrath was her masseur, Stephen Twigg, who was given the boot in July 1992 after opening his mouth to the press once too often.

Diana seems to have little patience with employees who are less than perfect—perfect, that is, as she defines it. In a 1987 interview published in *Woman* magazine, Diana's brother, Charles, Viscount Althorp, explained that his sister had managed to "weed out" many of the unproductive hangers-on who had been surrounding her and Charles. At about this same time, allegations surfaced that some of the people whom Diana had dismissed had been let go because they were gay. Unofficial tradition has placed gays in many royal staff jobs because they do not have spouses or children who may make demands on their time away from the royal family. Diana's rumored

Diana's royal duties are extensive. On her 1991 visit to Pakistan, for example, she was made an honorary member of the Chitral Scouts.

Even though her visit with Pope Paul II went very well, Diana was apparently extremely nervous about going to the Vatican to meet the Pope.

antipathy toward the whole idea was not good for her image, and speculation grew when Charles's loyal valet, Stephen Barry, resigned not long after his master's wedding. The rumored reason?—Diana had been unhappy with the close attention Stephen had been paying to her husband.

Whether Diana's homophobia exists at all is almost beside the point; the fact is that numerous servants and staffers, gay and straight, have left their positions since Diana joined the family. Assistant private secretary Francis Cornish quit his job in 1984 to become high commissioner in Brunei, while household accountant Michael Colborne also left that same year. Diana's equerry, Lieutenant Commander Peter Eberle, who had been with Diana since 1983, left his position in 1986, and his short-lived replacement, Richard Aylard, was superseded by Lieutenant Commander Patrick Jephson. The latter then took over as Diana's assistant private secretary when Anne Beckwith-Smith left that post in 1990.

More significant was the 1983 departure of Diana's private secretary, Oliver Everett. A capable man, Everett had been assistant private secretary to Charles and had occupied a top position with the govern-

ment's foreign office before returning to England from Spain in order to work for Diana. Not unreasonably, he assumed he would have the job for life. He was installed in the position in July of 1981 at an annual salary of £16,000.

A happy, if rather modest, ending seemed to be in store for Everett, but then he and Diana began to clash on the nature of her schedule. The princess was struck by whim more often than Everett liked, forcing him to repeatedly explain to her that her time was accounted for a full half year in advance, and that changes were very, very difficult to accommodate. Diana countered by telling Everett that it was his job as private secretary to see that all necessary accommodations were carried out. Everett stuck to his guns and insisted that the royal schedule be adhered to. The result was that Diana gave him the cold shoulder and ignored him out of existence. Everett

Most people around the world think of Diana when they think of Britain's royal family. It's not surprising, since she is beautiful, approachable, and always friendly.

resigned (against Charles's wishes), by now unable to return to the foreign office and forced to accept a posting as librarian at Windsor Castle.

Another of Diana's private secretaries, Sir John Riddell, also quit because of the princess's fondness for last-minute schedule changes. It seems apparent that Diana is determined to maintain at least a shred of a normal existence, royal duty or not.

Many other royal family employees—cooks, cleaners, chauffeurs, and housekeepers—have stayed just a short while before leaving. Turnover in low-level staff positions does not pique the interest of the press, but a story did seem to be brewing in 1985, when Edward Adeane, private secretary and treasurer to both Charles and Diana, unexpectedly quit. The newspapers, aware that Adeane, a man of high pedigree, had worked happily for Charles since 1979, assumed that the split had been precipitated by the arrival of Diana.

The real truth may lie with the behavior of Charles, not Diana. As we've seen, the prince has a streak of obstinacy, which may finally have rubbed Adeane the wrong way. Tired of having the prince ignore his advice, and at odds with Charles over the Protestant prince's tradition-breaking plan to visit the Pope at the Vatican, Adeane probably felt his time had come. (A visit to a papal Mass, by the way, was vetoed by Queen Elizabeth, who felt that such a meeting could incite problems with the Church of England.)

So Diana, it seems, is off the hook for the departure of Edward Adeane. Another well-publicized departure, that of nanny Barbara Barnes, may also have been the doing of Charles, who demanded stricter child discipline than Barnes was prepared to give. In

Above: *Fun in the sun.* Opposite: *Picking up a bag of apples at Tesco's goceries store in Liverpool is a media event, with flashing cameras and smiling admirers.*

Diana enjoys spending time with her sisters, Lady Jane Fellowes (right), and Lady Sarah McCorquodale (left). For old time's sake, they paid a visit to their alma mater, the West Heath School, where they were greeted by a former teacher.

sum, the notion that Diana is wholly to blame for upsets and departures among royal staffers may be due mainly to the vivid imaginations of the tabloid editors.

Diana's life at Kensington Palace and other city venues is often wearying; she and her family enjoy a far more relaxed sort of existence at the royal residence at Highgrove, set in 353 acres of Gloucestershire countryside. Although cheekily dubbed "Highgrave" by bored staff members, this gracious mansion and lovely grounds provide the royals with much-needed serenity. Diana's living room, its walls covered with drawings and photographs of her aristocratic ancestors and friends, overlooks a garden. It's a gracious room, decorated with glass and enamel ornaments, and filled with records and ballet mementoes. Although Diana's private sanctuary, the room seldom hosts the princess's friends; most visitors are family members and important "official" guests from abroad.

Diana's days at Highgrove usually begin at about 7:00, with a 30-minute swim followed by breakfast

and a scan of the papers and mail. Shopping in the nearby towns of Tetbury and Bath is always a possibility, and always carefully monitored by Diana's security officers.

Provocatively, Camilla Parker-Bowles lives not far from Highgrove and is a frequent visitor on days when Diana is not around. Generally, though, royal life at this secluded retreat is quiet and undramatic. If no guests are about, Diana may enjoy a three-course dinner and then watch television.

Yet for all of the apparent serenity of Highgrove, it is an invisibly tense, high-security place, as witness the "panic button" in every room, omnipresent security cameras, and hidden infrared beams.

Swimming is a sport that Diana has participated in ever since she was a child. No one knows whether she still delights onlookers with the "Spencer Special" dives that she did as a youngster, but the princess still tries to swim daily.

High-Profile Princess

For all of this century and much of the one that preceded it, the British royal family was acutely aware that its survival depended in large part on the good graces of the British people. To that end, monarchs from Victoria to Elizabeth II have taken care to avoid alienating the population at large. Royal behavior has been closely monitored (with middling results), as has outward appearance. Apparel, in particular, has played a vital part in the royal image: appropriately stately for official functions and state occasions; sober and conservative in less formal moments; casual yet discreet for leisure. This course has been wise because, after all, it wouldn't do to offend the British people. And anyway, it's the taxpayers who pick up much of the tab for whatever it is the royals wear on their backs. Gaudy (and expensive) high fashion just wouldn't be received well at all.

At least, that was the reasoning before Diana became Princess of Wales. Although not model-thin when she became engaged to Charles, Diana was, at 5'10½", uncommonly tall and very pretty. In addition to her physical attributes, she carried herself

Diana's choice of hats has given the British millinery business a new lease on life. Prior to her arrival on the scene, the royal choice in headgear had been a source of national amusement.

with poise and grace, and had a natural charm and charisma that turned heads. Fashion designers could only look at her and dream.

During her engagement to Charles, Diana took the safe route with long skirts and high necklines. But when public adulation inspired Lady Diana to slim from a size 12 (U.S. size 10) to a svelte size 10 (U.S. size 8), her fashion sense popped into gear. Confident that she could go where no other royal figure had ever gone before, she began to assemble a team of fashion advisors. Lady Jane Spencer, Diana's sister and at one time an editorial assistant at *Vogue* magazine, introduced the future princess to fashion editor Anna Harvey, former model Grace Coddington, and beauty editor Felicity Clark.

The team's first key recommendation was that Diana contact David and Elizabeth Emanuel for an outfit to wear to her first official outing, a March 9, 1981, reception in aid of the Royal Opera House at Goldsmith's Hall in London. The Emanuels threw themselves into the task and created a revealing black

Diana wowed them at the Reagan White House during her 1985 visit to the United States.

John Travolta danced with the princess at the White House and could not say enough nice things about her. Diana is a very good dancer who loves to take a spin around the floor.

taffeta strapless dress that was practically guaranteed to have the sort of effect Diana was hoping for. Charles certainly liked it, for he happily warned the press photographers to get ready as he preceded his fiancée from the limousine. When Diana stepped into view, the crowd cheered, the photographers gasped, and the evening was filled with the sound of camera motor drives.

Diana had been bitten hard by the fashion bug. When she set out on her first overseas tour, to Australia in 1983, it was with 90 trunks containing outfits by 21 different designers. Clearly, Diana was leaving nothing to chance.

Australia was only the beginning. On subsequent tours, Diana wowed 'em wherever she went: Brazil, Belgium, the United Arab Emirates, the United States. Not simply stunning to look at, she was clever, too. While at a dance in Melbourne, Australia in 1985, for instance, Diana wore Queen Mary's necklace as a headband, to considerable acclaim. The following year, at the America's Cup ball, she showed up in a Murray Arbeid gown that had a black top half and flame-red bottom half; the dress

During her first tour of Wales in 1981, Diana wore red and green—the colors of Wales. The suit was a new one designed by Donald Campbell; the hat by John Boyd had been worn previously.

Diana wears many Catherine Walker suits, such as this one. A trick used by royals to keep their hems from blowing up in a breeze is to weigh them down.

was complemented by arm-length gloves, one red and the other black.

The princess's imaginative choices of hats held particular delight for fashion mavens, who had been bemoaning royal hats for years. Lowri Turner, fashion editor of the London *Evening Standard*, remarked, "Since the Queen and Queen Mother's hats are always awful, Diana's are the only ones with any fashion angle. As a result, they are the only ones which people are interested in acquiring for themselves, and when I was at Ascot recently there were still some wearing the same style of hat as she wore with her going-away outfit—green, with a feather in it, Robin Hood-style. Luton [north of London] is the center of England's hat manufacturing trade, and there's a saying in this business that if Princess Diana sneezes, Luton catches a cold!"

In relatively short order, then, Diana had progressed from *fashionable* to *fashion-maker*. She was a trendsetter who was emulated by thousands of women.

Great-looking clothes have been just part of the public Diana's fashion story. Thanks partly to an innate cosmetic sense, and thanks partly to expert advice, Diana has perfected a subtle yet meticulously refined technique of selecting and applying makeup. The royal makeup artist, Barbara Daly, has been a big help, and Diana has enjoyed celebrity suggestions, as well, most notably Elizabeth Taylor's knowing advice about eye liner.

Fashion editor Lowri Turner explained, "What Diana learned to do by the second half of the eighties was to simplify her style, to look smarter and more sophisticated. She is tall and slim, and so she can wear things very well. That's not to say that she dresses in a particularly sexy way—she doesn't—because she has to present the classic styles. . . . but for her role she dresses very well and I therefore think Diana is a very good ambassador for British fashion. Compared to the rest of the royals she is remarkably well dressed. . . ."

Unfortunately, there was a down side to all of this high-fashion excitement: Diana's clothes cost a fortune. By 1990, she had purchased more than 750 outfits, including about 100 evening gowns, from designers such as Victor Edelstein, Franco Moschino, Gini Fratini, and a host of other top couturiers. The total cost was about two million dollars. Even the tab for Diana's hairstyling was running about $18,000 a year.

Considering that the Princess of Wales is essentially an international diplomat with no clout in international affairs, those figures are impressive in the worst possible way. And they were made public at the worst possible time, as the people of Britain struggled through an economic recession. Although Diana's subjects continued to be fond of her, they had to look twice at her spending. And anyway, wasn't it the job of royalty to inspire the downtrodden? What was Diana doing by rubbing everybody's nose in her fabulous wealth?

The "damage control" unit of Buckingham Palace got wind of the grumblings and swung into action. Of late, official reports about Diana's activities have had relatively little to say about her shopping habits. Special care has been taken to emphasize that Diana loans much of her wardrobe and gives portions of

This 1989 picture of a smiling Diana shows her attending a ball held by the British Paraplegic Sports Society. Needless to say, her presence at this event made it a special evening.

No other royal wears clothes as well as Diana does. She has perfected her own style of eye-catching elegance that is famous all over the world.

it to her sisters—not a very convincing justification for spending millions on dresses, but at least it's a start toward minimizing public bad feeling.

The fashion fallout might have been much worse if not for Diana's ebullient public personality, which continues to charm her subjects. She looks happy when having dinner at Ménage à Trois; she's a delight at those fashionable watering holes in Soho and Covent Garden. The British people find Diana hard to resist.

The princess is especially irresistible when she decides to cut loose and have fun in her own way. At a Christmas show for the supporters of the Royal Ballet and Opera at the Royal Opera House in December 1985, Diana sneaked from the royal box while the show was in progress and walked on to the stage, astonishing her husband and eliciting roars of approval from the audience. She joined modern-dance star Wayne Sleep in a three-minute dance performance to Billy Joel's "Uptown Girl," a bit of fancy footwork that Sleep had choreographed and rehearsed with Diana in secret meetings at Kensington Palace. The real object of all of this was to give Charles a pre-Christmas present; it's doubtful he will ever forget it.

Diana's Royal Opera House appearance was not the first time she performed before an audience. The previous month she and Charles had been feted at a White House banquet thrown by President Reagan and his wife, Nancy. Diana, decked out in a blue, off-the-shoulder Victor Edelstein gown, met and mingled with the Reagans and a host of celebrity guests, including Leontyne Price, Clint Eastwood, Mikhail Baryshnikov, Tom Selleck, and John Travolta. President Reagan, Eastwood, and other male guests tentatively danced with Diana, but the floor cleared when everyone stopped to watch Travolta put the princess through her paces to the accompaniment of "You're the One that I Want," a hit song from the actor's 1978 film, *Grease*. The couple danced for 15 minutes, to the delight of the onlookers and of Travolta himself, who happily asserted later that Diana had made him feel "like a prince."

Diana has made a point in recent years to balance her lighthearted image with a more sober one, mainly with high-visibility charity work (which will be discussed in the next chapter). But although she has moderated her image, her robust spending continues. Her health, beauty, and fashion needs require nearly half a million dollars a year. That's a lot of money, but then, she is president or patron of scores of worthwhile organizations and has endured a grueling public-appearance schedule since her marriage.

It is all of these factors, then, that the public must weigh and consider. A vibrant woman and a unique symbol of a great nation, Diana gives as good as she takes. Her fancies and diversions have not come cheaply, but neither has she charged for her tireless dedication to good causes or for the enormous amounts of energy she puts forth to advance the image of Great Britain around the world.

There were people who criticized Diana's extensive wardrobe, especially during recessionary times in England. These days she is sometimes seen in the same outfit more than once.

The Quality of Mercy: Diana's Charitable Endeavors

By visiting a place called Broadmoor in 1990, Diana did something no member of the royal family had ever done. Her purpose was to make clear to the public that people who suffer from mental disorders require and deserve treatment. That Diana chose Broadmoor to make her point (she returned in 1991 for a second visit) says a lot about her dedication to many charitable causes, for Broadmoor is a top-security prison hospital that houses many of Britain's most psychotic and violent criminals.

The significance of Diana's gesture is not that she placed herself in a position of modest risk, but that she chose to make her point in dramatic, even startling, fashion. Wherever she sees suffering, she will be present to help. If help is most likely to arrive after a high-profile gesture that will garner considerable press coverage, then that's the way Diana will do it.

In the early part of Diana's association with the royal family, her charitable work was a way to justify her existence to the British taxpayers, and a way for her to fill her time. But as her marriage collapsed around her, she turned to her charitable endeavors as

The Princess of Wales makes an incredible number of royal public appearances each year. Her visit to the Ormerod School in Oxfordshire brought a smile to her face and to the faces of those whom she came to visit.

a vehicle through which to find personal fulfillment and meaning in her life. No longer an unfocused, unambitious teenager, she does work that helps others, and that puts forth an image with which she can live comfortably. Diana is good-hearted and sensitive by nature. Her devotion to charity is deep and very real; besides being president of the Great Ormond Street Hospital for Sick Children, the Royal Marsden Hospital, the National Meningitis Trust, and the General Council and Register of Osteopaths, Diana is also a "patron" to about 40 more charitable organizations based in the United Kingdom and abroad. These deal with a wide variety of social and humanitarian problems.

Diana's position as patron of Relate, an organization designed to assist men and women involved in difficult relationships at home and in the workplace, is one in which Diana finds particular value. People who seek help from Relate suffer a variety of problems: ineffective communication with others; in-

Since her teenage days as a schoolgirl, Diana was very fond of elderly people and had a knack of talking to them. These wheelchair-ridden elderly women in Canada were quite impressed with their visitor.

70

Early in her life as princess, Diana became involved with an organization called Help the Aged. Her association with this charity has turned it into one of the most successful in the world.

ability to overcome childhood trauma; feelings of rootlessness; failing marriages. Given Diana's own background and marriage, it's no wonder that Relate chairwoman Zelda Westmeads remarked, "I think Diana is no different from other people; the more you learn about relationships and what makes people tick, the more you will gain in learning to deal with your own relationships, and I therefore think that she will have benefited from her work with us."

Each year Diana attends one or two film premieres that raise money for Relate. In addition, she makes about half a dozen visits each year to centers selected from the 130 that the organization maintains throughout Britain. She observes firsthand how the centers operate, and has an opportunity to meet and talk with people who are helped by the service. Relate chairwoman Zelda Westmeads revealed, "In [the eastern city of] Hull, recently, [Diana] sat in on a group session on helping victims of domestic violence, and on another occasion she joined a group of women who had been sexually abused as children and were suffering problems in their adult lives as a result. She does feel very caring and very able, despite who she is, to put people at their ease."

Diana has been involved in charity work since shortly after her engagement to Charles. She was dutiful from the start, and did her share of traveling, speaking, and hand-shaking. Many of her charitable activities culminated in glitzy social events designed to garner loads of publicity and encourage well-heeled guests to make hefty donations.

Then, as Diana's relationship with Charles ran aground, she threw herself into the work with new enthusiasm. She devoted herself to serious study of each cause and function, reading every word of assessment reports instead of just skimming them; immersing herself in facts, figures, and—most tellingly—the human side of each charity.

Diana understands that charities depend upon successful fund-raising. Her endorsement is of immense value, but she never wanted to be just a figurehead.

Many people feel that being with the disadvantaged and needy is depressing. Fortunately for these disabled children, the princess finds such work inspiring and joyous.

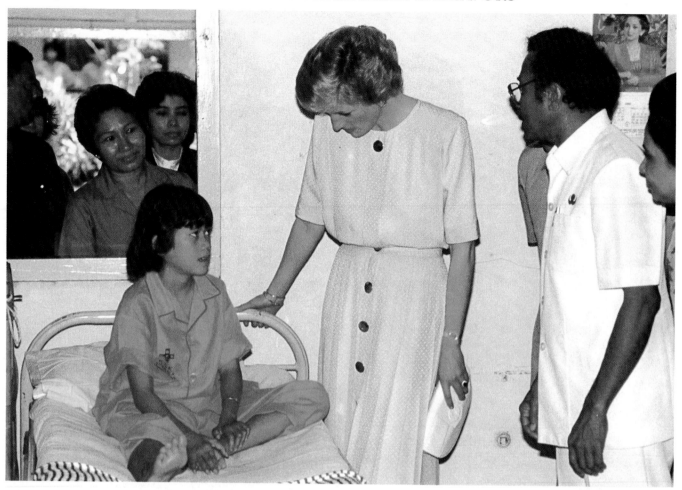

Diana's involvement with the sick is not limited to visits in her own country. Here she calls on a sick little girl in an Indonesian hospital.

Her job is to motivate others to give. She knows that she can do the most good if her activity on the charity's behalf expresses the story to the public in human terms. So it is that Diana jumps at opportunities to bring to the public the people who so desperately need help. When Britons see the victims of abuse and illness being warmly greeted by Diana, they make donations.

It's true that many who donate to Diana's causes do so because of self-interest; they may attend well-publicized charitable functions out of a desire to be seen with the princess and to have a good time, rather than because of a real wish to help others. But in the end, when the money is counted and sent to the administrators of each charity, the motives of those who have made donations really don't matter. Only the good work of the charity is important.

A loving mother, Diana surprised no one when she showed a particular interest in children's charities. As patron of the Pre-School Playgroups Association, she plays a vital role in raising the £55 million that is required annually to run the organization's 14,000 playgroups, where care is given to 600,000 British girls and boys under the age of five. To dramatize the existence of the organization and the children it serves, Diana has visited a number of the playgroups and has invited youngsters to tea parties at Kensington Palace. More than just a thrill for the lucky children, these events garner publicity and bring in much-needed money.

One of the first children's charities with which Diana became involved was the Malcolm Sargent Cancer Fund for Children, founded in 1968 and named for the noted conductor who died of the disease. The princess became a patron in 1982 and has attended many concerts and other fund-raisers on the organization's behalf.

Infant causes, too, occupy much of Diana's time. She has committed herself to numerous organizations that look after infants and toddlers, most no-

Diana works very hard for her charitable causes. In a single morning she will often visit three or four different charities during a royal tour. In 1984 this included some time spent in Salisbury.

74

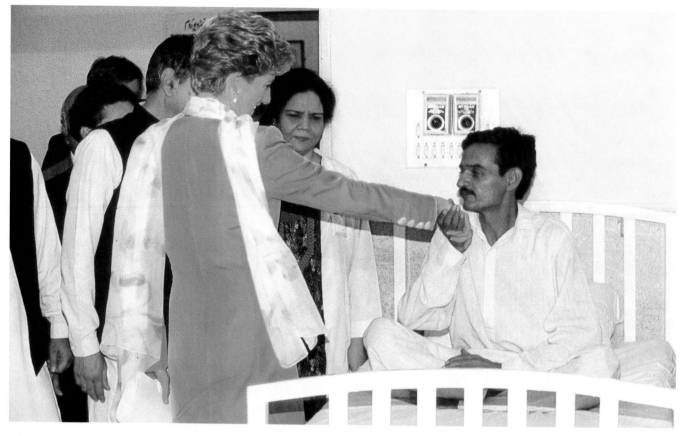

The princess's work with AIDS has become famous all over the world, as she tries to promote education about this horrible illness. She is not afraid to give an ungloved hand to this AIDS victim in Lahore, Pakistan.

tably Dr. Barnardo's, founded by a conscientious physician in 1866 and associated for many years with homes for orphans. Today, Barnardo's is Britain's largest child-care charity; over the years, many public figures, including Diana's friend, fashion designer Bruce Oldfield, have promoted the organization by publicly reminiscing about their own childhood experiences with Barnardo's.

Diana became president of the organization in 1984 and later became royal president of Barnardo's, Australia, and international president of Barnardo's, New Zealand. She makes regular visits to Barnardo's sites and attends functions almost monthly. In 1989, Barnardo's launched "If You Let Me," an ambitious campaign to help mentally disabled youngsters find jobs and places to live. The organization turned to Diana for help. She obliged by inviting three such youngsters to visit her at Kensington Palace, where she met the media and signed the campaign charter.

On the surface, Diana's genteel involvement in Barnardo's and other causes may seem trivial, even ineffectual, but to believe that, one must completely overlook the power of the princess's face and name in Great Britain. Cultural observers long ago coined the phrase "opinion maker," and that's precisely what Diana is to her subjects.

Her influence can be felt on the individual level, too, when a sincere chat and a handshake or hug boost the self-esteem of an ill or disadvantaged person. In all, Diana's message is clear and aimed at all of Great Britain: If the Princess of Wales is concerned about these people, the public should be concerned.

To effectively rouse public support is often challenging for even the most widely accepted causes; Diana goes the extra mile by aligning herself in the fight for victims of leprosy, AIDS, alcoholism, drug addiction, and mental illness—all of which carry unfairly heavy social stigmas. By doing so, Diana has shouldered a burden that many fund-raisers simply avoid.

She is patron of the Freshfield Service for drug counseling, the Institute for the Study of Drug Dependence, and, most important in her mind, Turning Point, which provides day care, counseling, and other services to people who suffer from mental illness,

On a recent trip to Hungary in 1992, Diana seemed to temporarily forget her own problems when she greeted old and young alike. Bringing joy to others seems to bring happiness to her.

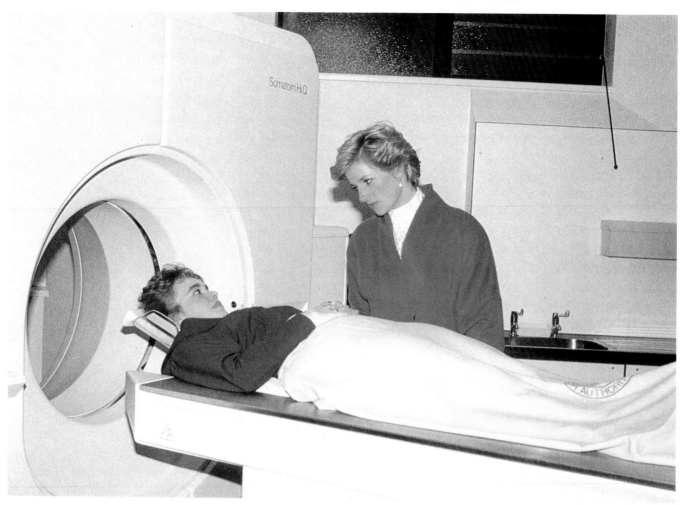

Medical tests can be quite scary, but a visit from a princess helps make the ordeal a little less painful. Appropriately, this hospital was named The Princess of Wales Hospital in Diana's honor.

alcoholism, and drug dependency. Diana has aggressively suggested that increased community care for troubled people will go a long way toward attacking the cause of such problems.

Public misconception about mental illness and substance abuse is formidable, but the myths and unreasonable fears that surround leprosy and AIDS are positively daunting. Not surprisingly, Diana views this as a challenge, and has jumped in with both feet, determined to educate the public about these illnesses, and raise money to help the victims.

Diana and Charles visited a leper colony in Nigeria in 1990, but it is the princess's solo campaign on behalf of AIDS victims that is particularly dramatic—and effective. Diana has been patron of Britain's National AIDS Trust since 1991, and has devoted herself to the opening of new wards, visits with doctors and patients, and participation in counseling sessions. Although increasing numbers of people are realizing that AIDS cannot be transmitted by a handshake or from a doorknob or by breathing the same air, not all people are willing to believe the facts. Diana,

aware that persistent ignorance is terribly damaging, made headlines in 1987 when she opened the AIDS unit at London's Middlesex Hospital and offered her uncovered hand to patients. She excited the press again two years later during a visit to Europe's first AIDS hospice, at Mildmay Mission in East London. And later in 1989, the princess made headlines in Britain and America, and won countless friends and admirers, when she hugged and played with seven children dying of AIDS in the pediatric unit of Harlem Hospital in New York City. The hospital's director, Dr. Margaret Heagarty, thanked the princess heartily, and was quick to publicly note that America's own leaders had done nothing to correct public misconceptions about AIDS. The symbolism

Carrying the now-familiar bouquet given to her by her adoring fans, the Princess of Wales visits yet another family clinic. Her presence always draws a huge crowd.

Diana's visit to Mildmay Mission Hospice in November of 1991 impressed the AIDS patients there. Her sympathy and compassion were evident as she tried to comfort the unfortunate people who were afflicted with this incurable disease.

of Diana's act, said Dr. Heagarty, was unique in America's battle against the awful ailment.

The most moving moment in Diana's public crusade on behalf of victims of AIDS came in 1991 at London's Middlesex Hospital. American First Lady Barbara Bush, well-liked in her own right, was present as Diana chatted with one of the patients. When the man suddenly began to cry, Diana gathered him into her arms and embraced him. This loving, spontaneous gesture coaxed tears from many who witnessed it.

It is abundantly clear to most observers that Diana is no dilettante, no mere dabbler in unhappy lives. She is not required to meet terminally ill people; she does not have to entertain handicapped children— she *chooses* to. At times, she becomes emotionally involved with the people she meets, and when informed later of a particular person's death, she will personally write a consoling note to the bereaved rel-

atives. Diana does not make such gestures public, and certainly does not make them out of a desire for good press, but they have come to light when grateful recipients of her words of sympathy and encouragement have shared the event with the media.

Diana herself has been one of the bereaved, and has had to confront AIDS on a very personal level. In 1991 she helped to look after her friend, Adrian Ward-Jackson, an AIDS patient who was in the ailment's latter stages. Ward-Jackson had been governor of the Royal Ballet, chairman of the Contemporary Arts Society, and director of the Theatre Museum Association. A month after receiving a CBE (Commander of the Order of the British Empire) medal at Buckingham Palace for his tireless work in the arts, his condition became critical. From that point, Diana was frequently at his bedside at his home and at St. Mary's Hospital in London.

When a mutual friend phoned Diana at Balmoral to let her know that Ward-Jackson had just hours to live, the princess drove 600 miles with a bodyguard (no flights were immediately available) to the hospital, where she arrived at 4:00 A.M. She maintained a vigil at her friend's bedside for the next three days. When Adrian Ward-Jackson died on August 23, 1991, Diana could take solace in the fact that she had performed as a friend should: quickly, selflessly, with love. For Diana, Princess of Wales, charity truly does begin at home.

Strength in adversity seems to be Diana's motto. Here she once again visits patients at Elgar House at Southmead Hospital. Few people seem to devote as much time to the infirm as the Princess of Wales does.

Diana's work with AIDS has made headlines. She devotes time to opening new wards, visits with doctors and patients, and participates in counseling sessions.

Diana's Search for a Happy Ending

As Diana continued her public appearances and charitable work in the early part of 1992, the royal family's troubles escalated. In March, Sarah Ferguson, the Duchess of York, formally separated from Prince Andrew. The British tabloid press, which had built "Fergie" up to dizzying heights, turned against her with a vengeance. It was not simply the separation that the press was responding to, but a culmination of many things: Prince Andrew's spray-paint vandalism of American photographers' camera equipment; Prince Edward's ill-advised participation in a slapstick TV game show; startling allegations that the father of Princess Michael of Kent had been a Nazi SS officer; and, of course, Charles and Diana's disintegrating marriage.

Royal observer Margaret Holder asserted, "There's no soap opera I know of which could compare to the bizarre situation that the House of Windsor is in now. Not even *Dynasty* at its height. Every day some other facet is appearing. . . . the royals are going to have to adapt, or there will be such a public outcry that Parliament will have to act. . . . The big question is whether Charles is fit to become king. If he did [become king], I don't believe any government of the day would get on with him."

So there it was: public speculation about Charles's fitness to rule. It had all finally caught up with

The death of her father was one of many misfortunes that plagued the unhappy princess in 1992. Opposite: More and more current photos show an unhappy Diana and Charles. Many people wonder if the royal couple will be able to maintain a cordial front in public for much longer.

Charles and Diana—the ceaseless press coverage of their predicament, the photos of a clearly miserable Diana, the publicity surrounding Andrew Morton's book, *Diana: Her True Story*. Buckingham Palace reeled beneath the onslaught and was forced to swing into its damage-control mode in the spring and summer of 1992. A strategy was needed, and it was needed right away.

The queen and Prince Charles met at Buckingham Palace on June 12. There had been other unsympathetic books about the monarchy, of course, but none had been as bold as Morton's, and none had arrived at a moment of incipient family crisis. Elizabeth and Charles worried not only about the future of the royal couple, but about the future of the whole royal family.

Charles and his mother decided that he had three options. One strategy would be for him to completely ignore Morton's book and the accompanying press coverage, and to go on as if nothing at all were amiss. A second option would have Charles step up his personal appearances in order to gain increased public sympathy. The prince's third option would be to come out fighting, to tell his side of the story, encourage his friends to publicly attack Diana, and reestablish himself as a leader.

Of these choices, the first was the weakest and riskiest. In all likelihood, a "What? Me worry?" ap-

83

The Duke and Duchess of York, Sarah and Andrew, announced in March of 1992 that they want to terminate their marriage. The very popular Fergie of a few years ago became the tabloid reporters' chief object of scorn after the announcement.

proach would simply anger the public and lead to an even greater brouhaha than the present one.

The second option, while it would probably be successful in boosting the prince's image, would do nothing to address his messy marriage, and certainly would not guarantee his ascension to the throne if he were to divorce. In fact, that ascension would be nearly impossible because the monarch is the head of the Anglican Church, which does not approve of divorce. Only one divorced person had ever succeeded to the British throne, George I, and that had happened about 300 years ago.

Charles's third option, to defend himself and have his friends attack Diana, would make him look assertive, all right, but could also finish off the marriage for good. Once again, the prince would be faced with the sticky politics of divorce.

There was a loophole, but it was a small one: With permission from the queen—in negotiation with the prime minister—or the Privy Council, Charles could remarry, but such permission would be unlikely.

It is ironic, yet somehow not surprising, that Diana was not present at this first crisis meeting. Blood, it seems, is thicker than a lot of things, in-

cluding marriage. However, Diana was present at the second damage-control meeting, which was held three days later, on June 15, at Windsor Castle. This meeting also included Prince Philip, who had been away during the first strategy session. The four royal personages locked themselves away inside the recesses of the castle and decided that divorce was out of the question. Instead, Diana and Charles would enter into a six-month "cooling-off" period in which they would emphasize joint public appearances and put on happy faces for the media and public. This stopgap measure would hold the marriage together, at least temporarily, but would not do a thing to spruce up Charles's image.

That problem was addressed the following week, in a meeting of the prince and his advisers (once again, poor Diana was conspicuous by her absence).

The 1986 wedding of Fergie and Prince Andrew appeared to be such a happy time in the life of the royal family. The happiness did not last long, however, as their marriage disintegrated.

It is up to Queen Elizabeth and her husband, Prince Philip, to come up with a plan to either save the marriage of Charles and Diana or to offer a way out that would be acceptable to all concerned parties.

The group arrived at a four-point plan that represented a compromise between the three options that had been discussed at the first meeting on June 12.

First, a carefully orchestrated public relations campaign to emanate from Buckingham and Kensington palaces would focus on Charles's devotion to his duties, his love of Britain, and his deep concern for the environment.

Second, it would be revealed that, while the prince's friends were up in arms about his ill treatment at the hands of the press, they were remaining silent at his request, "for the sake of the children."

The plan's third point was a carefully orchestrated one in which the prince's friends, unable to contain their indignation a moment longer, would recount his side of the story to the media. Every story would be given to the press anonymously, in order to lessen the prince's distress about his friends acting against his wishes.

The final point of the plan was the most scurrilous of all: All of Charles's problems, and the problems of the marriage, would be laid at Diana's feet. The ra-

tionale for this bit of legerdemain would be that the princess's bulimia had set off her depressions and unreasonable behavior. Her refusal to be treated for the disorder had only aggravated the situation. In other words, everything that had gone wrong in the marriage was Diana's fault, but she wasn't really responsible because of illness. In a single stroke, then, much of the unfavorable impact of Andrew Morton's book would be lessened.

The plan seemed neat, clever, and inexcusably crass. It could have been lifted from an old movie—the familiar plot twist of the essentially innocent victim who is chosen to take the fall.

The palace put the first three points of the plan into simultaneous operation on June 28, 1992, with a full-page article that appeared in the *Sunday Times*

Through all of the personal problems and embarrassments that the royal family has experienced in recent times, the queen must maintain the dignity of the House of Windsor in the eyes of the British people.

under the headline, "The Case for Charles." The article was accompanied by a large photograph of the prince, cheerfully shaking hands with his subjects during one of his public appearances. Surprisingly, the article revealed much of what had been discussed at the crisis meetings, then went on to name a few of Charles's friends who had spoken to the article's writers on his behalf, but who declined to be quoted on the record. The list was an impressive one that included ex-King Constantine of Greece; Charles's confidante, Candida Lycett-Green; his hunting companion Didi Saunders; and the prince's cousin, Lord Romsey, and his wife, Countess Mountbatten.

The article also contained unattributed quotes from "friends" of the prince who acknowledged that, yes, the royal marriage was in trouble, but that the Charles described in Morton's book was not the Charles they knew. In addition, some of these anonymous supporters mentioned specific incidents in Morton's book, recounting them for the article in a different light, one that showed Charles far more sympathetically.

The final element of the four-point plan, the one that cast Diana as the villain of the piece, was put

Top: *Ever since he was born, Prince Charles was groomed to someday be the king of England.* Above: *Diana and Charles enjoyed King Fahd's state visit. There certainly did not appear to be any strain between the two of them.* Right: *Many of us like to remember Charles and Diana as they appeared on their honeymoon. They were smiling, happy, and very much in love. How quickly their feelings changed!*

The Prince and Princess of Wales have traveled all over the world. Each trip requires an amazing amount of preparation as clothes need to be made and bought, staff prepared, appointments set up, and presents purchased.

into action on July 6, when Britain's *Today* newspaper kicked off a series of articles called "Charles: *His* True Story." The series was "specially researched and prepared" by Penny Junor, one of the prince's biographers, who claimed that she had been asked by Charles's friends to set the record straight.

The series trotted out still more anonymous, pro-Charles accounts. Many of these unnamed participants expressed anger at the way in which the royal couple's "most private secrets" had been revealed and turned against the prince in a conspiratorial way.

These same anonymous sources introduced the palace's spin on Diana's bulimia, claiming that its origins lie in the princess's unhappy childhood, and that the side effects of the condition caused problems in the royal relationship "before the first night of marriage."

From this unpromising beginning, Junor's portrait of Diana quickly became almost completely unsympathetic. The articles claimed that Charles adored his sons and wanted to spend time with them, but was prevented by Diana from doing so. Junor reported that when Charles tried to find help for his

wife, Diana had responded with "tears and shouting."

Junor also addressed Charles's relationship with Camilla Parker-Bowles by saying that the prince's longtime friend had helped him to "maintain his sanity in a traumatic marriage." According to the palace's strategy, then, Camilla was far from a disruptive influence; to the contrary, she was helping to hold Charles (and, by implication, a major part of the monarchy) together.

British national television and radio embraced Junor, who elaborated on the points she had made in the *Today* articles. Of all of her remarks that went over the airwaves, the most telling was her assertion that, although the royal marriage had been badly damaged, it could be saved *if* Diana sought treatment

Princess Diana appears so haggard and unhappy. We can only speculate whether the reason behind her apparent unhappiness is travel fatigue or personal problems.

for her illness. If she did that, Charles would be willing to give the marriage another chance.

Clearly, the palace strategy was to paint Charles as not just abused but magnanimous; and to reveal Diana as not just disturbed, but childish and petulant.

Does Diana have any hope for happiness at all? Will she find that elusive happy ending? That her husband and the rest of the royal family don't really care whether she does or not is abundantly clear, and crushingly sad. Diana can expect little help from her husband, and even less from those who contrive with him to manipulate his image.

If Diana opts out of the marriage, her sons, princes William and Harry, will remain heirs to the throne. Diana would retain her title as Princess of Wales, but her royal duties would almost certainly cease. Should she remarry, she would forfeit the title as well as any income arrived at in a divorce settlement. In all, a bleak option, but one that would at least allow Diana to retain her self-respect and peace of mind.

Top: *Being a member of the royal family is not easy duty. During their trip to Italy, Diana was criticized for her choice of clothes.* Above: *The Princess of Wales enjoys dancing; the prince does not. This time duty called.* Right: *If Charles and Diana divorced, her royal duties would most certainly cease.*

If Diana chooses to remain in the marriage, she and Charles would lead separate lives and would come together in private only as part of their obligations to their sons. Otherwise, Diana and her husband would be together only for public appearances and official functions. Barring reconciliation, it would be a lonely existence, particularly for Diana, who would continue to live beneath the harsh glare of public scrutiny.

Could Diana thrive under such a lifetime arrangement? Would she want to carry on at all, knowing how Charles and the palace had conspired to point fingers at her? And would a sham of a marriage hoodwink the British people? Would they be gratified by such transparent role-playing? Does Britain deserve better than that?

Top: *If the prince and princess remain married but lead separate lives, they would only come together for official functions. The relationship would probably be chilly, formal, and unsatisfying, particularly for Diana.* Right: *Being under the eye of the cameras and public scrutiny is a difficult situation to be in for Diana. Although she has been the object of keen interest for more than ten years, Diana has never been quite comfortable with the situation.* Far right: *Will Charles and Diana ever be able to recapture that elusive happiness that once was theirs?*

Only Charles, Diana, and a few palace insiders know whether this happy family unit will remain intact or not. The resolution will have very real political consequences for Britain.

The tidal wave of rumor and speculation may taper off in time, but it will surely continue to be a part of Diana's life. And none of it will mean a thing because only Diana can know her own mind. Her thoughts and emotions are hers alone, and only she can answer the questions that haunt her. She is the fairy-tale princess who needs a happy ending.

Of course, not every fairy tale celebrates a beautiful young woman who meets her prince. There is another fairy-tale tradition, a darker one, that places innocence in peril; a tradition of lost children, hungry wolves, and witches who lurk within candy cottages. Yet even in these grim little stories, so full of peril and menace, virtue triumphs. In the end, goodness wins.